"Written by a knowledgeable parent and skilled educator, the SCHOOL SAVVY KIDS series belongs on every parent's bedside table."

—BRENDA NIXON, M.A.

speaker; author of *Parenting Power in The Early Years*

"Thank you, Cheri, for meeting moms and dads right where they are—for pushing away the negative issues of parenting and replacing them with practical hope!"

—LAURIE LOVEJOY HILLIARD AND SHARON LOVEJOY AUTRY

speakers, Mom and Loving It conferences

SCHOOL STARTS AT HOME

simple ways to make learning fun

cheri fuller

school savvy kids

OUR GUARANTEE TO YOU

We believe so strongly in the message of our books that we are making this quality guarantee to you. If for any reason you are disappointed with the content of this book, return the title page to us with your name and address and we will refund to you the list price of the book. To help us serve you better, please briefly describe why you were disappointed. Mail your refund request to: Piñon Press, P.O. Box 35002, Colorado Springs, CO 80935.

© 2004 by Cheri Fuller

All rights reserved. No part of this publication may be reproduced in any form without written permission from Piñon Press, P.O. Box 35007, Colorado Springs, CO 80935. www.pinon.org

Published in association with the literary agency of Alive Communications, Inc., 7680 Goddard Street, Suite 200, Colorado Springs, Colorado, 80920.

PIÑON PRESS and the PIÑON PRESS logo are registered trademarks of Piñon Press. Absence of ® in connection with marks of Piñon Press or other parties does not indicate an absence of registration of those marks.

ISBN 1-57683-600-2

Cover photography by Corbis
Cover design by David Carlson Design
Creative Team: Rachelle Gardner, Arvid Wallen, Cara Iverson, Glynese Northam

Content originally included in *Home-Life: The Key to Your Child's Success at School,* by Cheri Fuller, Honor Books, 1988.

Some of the anecdotal illustrations in this book are true to life and are included with the permission of the persons involved. All other illustrations are composites of real situations, and any resemblance to people living or dead is coincidental.

Fuller, Cheri.
  School starts at home : simple ways to make learning fun / Cheri Fuller.
      p. cm. -- (School savvy kids)
  Includes bibliographical references (p.   ) and index.
  ISBN 1-57683-600-2
  1. Early childhood education--Parent participation. 2. Home schooling. I. Title. II. Series.
  LB1139.35.P37F85 2004
  372.21--dc22
                                        2004004253

Printed in Canada

1 2 3 4 5 6 7 8 9 10 / 08 07 06 05 04

To my grandchildren Caitlin and Caleb Fuller

contents

acknowledgments

Thanks to Rhana Robison, Dr. Margaret Loeffler, Dr. Charles and Sue Gouaux, Dr. Lauren Bradway, Karen Gale, Sally Conway, Dr. Dale Jordan, Dr. Diana Waters, and Dr. Eugene Walker for their insights and suggestions on children and learning. My thanks also to a special group of teachers and mothers who shared their experiences and suggestions: Patti Milburn, Lynn Fuller, Carole Ashmore, Shirley Pugh, Jerry Gautreaux, Kay Bishop, Marilyn Morgan, Melanie Hemry, Joanna Smith, Corrie Sargeant, Cynthia Morris, Joyce Findley, Vicki Hamilton, Dana Smith, Vivian Nida, Freeda Richardson, Diana Purser, and Candy Snowbarger.

I'm grateful for the teachers who encouraged me throughout my learning journey, especially two of the best: my first-grade teacher, Mrs. Julia Rogers Taylor; and Nan Carpenter at Garland High School, whose comment "lucid writing" on my essays sparked hope.

Heartfelt thanks to my editor, Rachelle Gardner, for her skills and ideas for this book. Also, thanks to the Piñon staff for their love for kids and desire to encourage families.

Most of all, I am grateful for my parents, George and Mildred Heath, who gave me a home life and heritage that nurtured a love of learning. Thanks to my lifelong learning companion and dear husband, Holmes; our grown children and their spouses—Justin and Tiffany, Chris and Maggie, Alison and Hans; and our grandchildren, from whom I have learned so much.

the power of

parental involvement

Carrie and Jack's daughter Katie is four years old, and they want to help her get the best foundation for learning before she begins kindergarten. Katie is verbal, inquisitive, and high-spirited, and her parents have great expectations for her. They wonder how they can help her live up to her potential—without putting on too much pressure.

Patty decided to homeschool her children, ages seven and nine. She finds it's sometimes challenging to motivate her kids to be eager learners every day, but she's always on the lookout for the best ways to help her kids learn. Most of all, she wants to find ways to integrate learning into their everyday lifestyle at home.

Heather's son Jason, now in the third grade, often forgets to bring his books home, procrastinates on doing homework, and is struggling in math and social studies. His mom found school frustrating in her growing-up years, so she wants education to be more rewarding and positive for Jason. This kid really needs a turnaround! Heather wonders what she can do to help Jason enjoy learning.

Maybe you identify with Carrie and Jack, Patty, or Heather. The good news is that as a parent, you can have a huge positive impact on your children's education. What you do and how you're involved in your kids' learning has more influence on their attitude and achievement than anything any other person does. Your home environment can become one that supports the learning process in positive and long-lasting ways.

Learning starts at home, and no matter what kind of schooling option you choose, you are your children's first and most important educator. And even if you delegate part of your kids' learning to a school, you are still the director of the whole long-term, twelve-plus-years process. More than fifty research studies show that when parents get involved in their children's learning, their kids are more motivated, get their needs met more effectively, and score significantly higher on achievement tests than kids with parents who are uninvolved.

Over and over, I've seen that when parents take an active role in their children's learning, the results are dynamic. Studies of successful kids reveal parents who are actively engaged in helping their children throughout their school years, even in simple ways. When parents are good role models and enjoy learning, showing an interest in what their children are learning by asking questions, students get more inspired and achieve higher grades. When parents know their kids well, they can better help them bypass their weaknesses and amplify their strengths so they can function at their best in the classroom.

As a former teacher who has taught students at every grade level from kindergarten to college, I've spoken to hundreds of parents and teachers. I've given them ideas to support their children's learning, turn around negative attitudes, and help their kids get the most out of the school experience, whether they are being educated at home or at a public or private school. I've seen parents themselves get recharged with new ideas and strategies that make a huge difference in their children's learning.

Most parents want to be involved in their children's schoolwork and to see their kids succeed, but many don't know what to do or where to start. That's why I wrote this book. Through those years of teaching, I began to realize that we parents are the ones who really need the encouragement and help. The key to our children's lifelong learning and success in school lies in the quality of their home lives, not only during the important first five years of their lives but throughout their entire school experience.

In this book, I'll share with you some simple tools to help you develop a home environment that is rich in learning resources and foundational for an excellent education for your children. You'll discover how to:

- Integrate fun learning activities into daily life

- Help your children become lifelong writers and readers

- Teach your kids simple study strategies and organizational skills that will multiply their retention and raise their grades

- Enhance your children's learning and development with music

- Communicate with school personnel, solve problems that arise, and engage in an effective conference with a teacher

- Encourage your kids to keep learning during the summer

With the constant changes in technology and knowledge, we can't teach kids all the facts and formulas they will need to know in order to succeed in life. But if we can help them learn to think critically, read and write well, and develop a lifestyle of learning, they'll continue to learn long after their formal education has ended.

You may be asking such questions as, *How long are these activities going to take?* and *How do you expect me to make time for these educational concerns in my already overcrowded schedule?* In this book, I'll give you ideas that can be incorporated into your lifestyle, whether you are a working or a stay-at-home parent. There are dozens of suggestions for things you can do with your children without becoming a taskmaster or holding a two-hour study hall every night. You'll discover ways to be a positive role model and teach by example, how your home life can support your children's development, and how to be an encourager and a homework coach to your children rather than doing the assignments yourself.

As you use these ideas, I think you'll find that the time you spend with your children in a learning activity will be multiplied back to you as your children grow to become more independent students during their junior high school and high school years. Reading aloud, discussing a newspaper article around the dinner table, and going on a family outing are all effective ways to build a foundation for them to become lifelong learners and successful in whatever paths they take.

One night when all three of our kids were in school, we'd just come back from the second night in a row of Open House. I'd spent my day volunteering at our daughter's school and helping one of our sons study for a test, and I was exhausted. I looked at my husband and exclaimed, "I can't believe what a huge part of our lives the kids' schooling is!" Yes, sometimes it's draining. But with some preparation, your kids' schooling can be a positive part of your life together rather than a source of stress.

Recently, I heard a mother say, "I'm not a teacher. I didn't even like school myself, so I don't have much to teach my children." Maybe you've felt the same way, but I want to make you realize that you have much to teach your children.

One evening, my young daughter, Alison, and I were riding bikes together. Alison was riding ahead of me on her new bicycle. As we went around the curves and onto a busy residential street, I coached her a little from behind. A car zoomed up behind me. "Stay a little closer to the right curb," I called out to her. A little later, "Better stop at the corner and look both ways," I cautioned. "Good job when you signaled to turn left!"

Supervising a child's education is much like that bike ride. The educational system is like a busy city street. Most kids need some personal coaching and a lot of encouragement if they are to get through it with positive results instead of calamity.

That's our job as parents. We can't ride the bike for our children, but we can coach them until they can maneuver through the busy street on their own and arrive safely at their destination. We can make sure they have the right equipment for the trip. We can know where they're going. We can help them up when they fall. We can even help them get a tire fixed when it goes flat.

This book will equip you to guide your children so that in spite of any problems they may face in school—whether public, home, or private—they will be prepared to learn, get the most out of what the school offers, and develop the skills needed to succeed.

Although many of my examples relate to moms, let's not forget the powerful impact fathers can have on forming a foundation for children's achievement. A dad's encouragement and support is a vital key for a child's learning, whether it's by reading aloud to the family, sharing projects and hobbies, showing an interest in school activities, or even being a volunteer.

As you read this book, choose the activities that fit in with your family's lifestyle and schedule. You can't do everything, but picking a few ideas to apply in your home will make a difference. While millions of dollars pumped into education often fail to raise children's achievement, I've found that a few small reforms made at home can show terrific results.

a stable home environment

Throughout your children's lives, you'll spend countless hours helping them learn. Whether it's tying shoes, telling time, shooting a free throw, or mastering multiplication tables, your children will be learning at a fast pace, and they'll need your help. Throughout the rest of this book, I'm going to share with you dozens of tips for getting kids through their school years. But the most important thing I want to emphasize—more critical than any amount of reading, music, sports, or art instruction—is that children learn best when they have a stable home environment.

The dictionary definition of *stability* includes:

■ Resistant to deterioration or displacement

■ Not likely to break down, fall apart, or give way

■ Firm, steady, not easily thrown off balance

■ Constancy of character or purpose

■ Capable of returning to equilibrium or original position after being shaken or displaced.[1]

Think about your family being like parts of a hanging mobile with you, the parents, being the larger pieces and your children the smaller pieces. When external or internal stresses occur, the pieces move. They are all affected by the shifting motion of the others. Stability is what gives your family the ability to maintain an even keel and return to the balanced position even after a jostling occurs.

How can you tell whether or not your home gives your children a feeling of stability? Over the years, I've noticed three specific situations that tend to rob the home of its stability:

- Constant time crunch

- Schoolwork anxiety and stress

- Family crisis, such as death, divorce, or relocation

Difficult circumstances do come unannounced and uninvited into all of our lives. But what can we as parents do to reestablish stability and support our kids so they can keep growing and learning when something happens to shake the family's security? Let's deal with these stability robbers one at a time.

do we have time?

Mom hurries in from work with a sack of groceries. Brian screeches by on his bike on his way to a friend's house. Upstairs, Jessica hurriedly dresses for ballet class, skips down the stairs three at a time to dash into the kitchen, and asks, "Mom, can you drive me to the dance studio?" At the same time, a tense Dad races home on the highway, knowing he will be home only forty-five minutes before he has to preside at the church's Adult Education committee meeting. Overcrowded lives, stressed parents, hurried children—do you ever have a night like this? We had far too many!

"I feel like I'm on a fast train and can't get off," said one mother. "My life is all bits and pieces."

"I wish we had some time for Dad and me to go camping," ten-year-old Michael confided.

"The only thing I want for Christmas is about two more weeks to get ready for it," lamented a harried mom of twins and a teenager as she came in from hours of running errands.

Most of us are zooming through life in fast-forward. Our kids lead sped-up lives as well. With schools cutting back on recess and lunch time, and extracurricular activities increasing, most of kids' waking hours are now packed with classes, homework, sports, lessons, and much more.

What happens to kids who are constantly rushed and whose days and minds are crammed? First, short-term memory is affected. Lots of stimulation without time to relax is like baking bread without giving it time to rise. When kids have downtime or are resting or sleeping, the brain creates the connections and long-term memory needed in the learning process. If a child's short-term memory is jumbled and rushed, then his mind doesn't build long-term memory patterns.

Too much outside stimulation also diverts and usurps interior energy. It's like trying to watch a DVD on fast-forward.

When things go too fast, kids may miss the meaning of what they hear. Their minds become like a bowl of peanuts—just bits and pieces—and they get disorganized. The combination of stress and hurry can rob children of vital reading, writing, and math skills. In order to build a long-term framework of knowledge, there needs to be a time each day when kids are quiet, settled, and reflective.

"A little bit of stress can be motivating, add interest, and keep arousal levels high enough to complete a task," said one researcher. But too much stress and pressure works against the learning process and can affect brain function. "When there is excess stress over the long term, the brain produces a chemical that disrupts working memory and reduces one's desire to explore new ideas and creatively solve problems."[2] Maybe one place to start in promoting your child's learning this year would be to reduce excess hurriedness in your family's life.

Make an effort to give your child some of your time each week—preferably each day—so she can just hang out and play or talk with you. When your attention is focused on her and truly "tuned in" to her needs, it helps reduce her stress and it's a tangible way to express your care. It helps build self-worth, establish communication, and create emotional closeness, and it's the very best way to fill up a young person's "emotional tank." When their emotional needs are met, children's behavior improves and learning increases.

Time together may be having a hamburger out with your child or throwing the football around and talking over the events of the day after school. It can be a walk around the block or stop-ping for a Coke on the way home from soccer practice. It could be just doing a puzzle or playing a game your child enjoys. Or perhaps the thirty minutes before bedtime is your favorite time to spend together.

After several decades of working with families and kids, Dr. Dale Jordan, a learning specialist and education professor, con-cluded that "the most important thing you can do for your child's education is to clear your calendar and be there during those formative years." He advised that as often as possible, we should come home in the evening; get relaxed; have a meal together; share the events of the day; and make time for homework, read-ing, and other shared activities.[3]

It takes some planning to help our kids plan their time between work, play, study, sleep, family time, and other activi-ties so there's balance in their lives. (It's hard enough to do this in our own lives!) When they are overscheduled and running from one activity to another, young people experience burnout just as adults do. Home becomes only a pit stop where clothes are changed and a glass of juice is gulped down on the way out the door. Kids need to have some unstructured time for play, think-ing, or rest in the family setting. Downtime gives them chances to explore, use their curiosity, think, daydream, or just be quiet.

Our home was as busy as anyone else's, and we certainly experienced hectic times when two basketball games, a tennis match, theater practice, a big meeting at work, and a friend's birthday party happened to fall on the same day. But if that becomes the norm and your child is showing signs of overcommitment, then it's time to intervene. Signs of overcommitment include headaches and stomach pain, frequent restlessness and tiredness, appearing depressed but not communicating feelings, losing interest in an activity that once was important, falling grades or decreased interest in schoolwork, antisocial behavior such as lying and stealing, and being more dependent on parents than in the past.

Here are some ideas to try that might help your child cope with stress or overcommitment:

- Assist your child in evaluating which activities are producing a problem.

- If she has too little free time, help her change her schedule to make room for relaxation and play.

- Spend time together with your child each day, even if for only fifteen minutes.

- Simplify your own schedule. If it is hectic or unmanageable, it can cause your child to be stressed or nervous about her activities.[4]

You might be forced to make some tough decisions. You really want her to have the advantage of both piano lessons and ballet class, but is it worth the time crunch it causes? Your athletic son may want to play soccer, hockey, and basketball, but is there really enough time in a week for all three? Some of your decisions may be unpopular, but you'll be teaching your child how to keep his life manageable—a skill he'll thank you for in the long run.

dealing with school stress

"School is hard for me. I get upset when I fail a test. I get real nervous when my teacher is mad at the class or when I do something wrong," said ten-year-old Courtney.

"I don't like to be called names by the other kids or be left out of games at recess," said one fourth-grade boy.

Lots of kids are upset about things at school: They're afraid of being bullied on the bus or playground, fearful of being intimidated or humiliated by a teacher, frustrated at making low grades, or preoccupied about problems with friends.

For some children, school is a positive, rewarding experience. They thrive in competitive situations and love the challenge of school. But for others, the competitive, test-oriented atmosphere is stressful. In large classes, it may be difficult to get their needs met. Some children feel as though they are being rushed from class to class and activity to activity throughout the school day. Many kids find classroom work repetitious and monotonous.

With today's increased emphasis on achievement and the higher standards imposed in schools comes more pressure. When more pressure is placed on them at school, children need correspondingly more support at home. Most kids respond better to hugs, kisses, and high fives than to pressure. Rather than sternly saying, "Get in there and study," try encouraging them warmly.

"We often put on more pressure than children can handle," said Dr. Eugene Walker, director of pediatric psychology training at the University of Oklahoma Medical School. "Schoolteachers are putting on pressure. Parents are saying to their child, 'You can do better, you must bring your grades up,' and express displeasure when not satisfied with the results. At the same time, parents might convey displeasure with the child and their relationship with the child. Children have a hard time disconnecting their performance from who they are as people. Promote and encourage, but avoid pressuring your child."[5]

He adds that for a while, students seem to do better under pressure, but it soon gets tiresome and they begin to experience burnout. Unless something is done to relieve the stress, they will eventually quit trying and drop out. Many capable students do great in elementary school—they turn in perfect papers, receive top grades, and take pride in accomplishment. But then in high school and college, their performance deteriorates.

Listening to our kids helps us discover the issues that distract them from learning. If your child seems troubled, ask some of the following questions: What's going on at school? What are you interested in? What is difficult about school? Do you have any enemies at school? Are you having any problems in your classwork? What are your happiest times at school?

Instead of comparing him to siblings or pushing him to catch up with classmates who are scoring higher, encourage him to compete with himself, and he'll begin to believe he can accomplish his own goals. To calm test fears in your sixth- or seventh-grader who's worried about passing a big test at the end of the year, put things in perspective by assuring him, "No, you won't be held back if you don't score well on this exam. You've worked hard all year!"

> *Total empathy is difficult to achieve, and no one can empathize with another person all the time. When we can, however, it means a great deal to our children. "Mom understands." "Dad understands." It feels good to be understood. It wipes out loneliness.*
>
> —CHARLOTTE SAWTELLE, *LEARNING IS A FAMILY AFFAIR*[6]

After we listen to the particular worries of our children, we can show empathy and understanding without condemning or judging. We can be physically supportive by hugging or holding them. We can give information, share feelings, and assure our kids that we are with them in their problems. We can let them know we had the same kind of problems when we were young. Sharing our past experiences and struggles gives them courage and hope that they can make it through too. We can suggest alternatives or offer to provide any extra help that may be needed, such as scheduling a conference with the teacher or school counselor.

You'll have to evaluate as you go: *Is my child in the right class or the right school? Is she getting the extra help she needs? Are her concerns being heard, acknowledged, and validated?*

If a learning gap or an academic deficiency is causing low grades or failure, a tutor may be able to help the child catch up. Many times, enormous strides can be made by one-to-one instruction. Also, study strategies can help kids cope with the challenges of school with less anxiety and more confidence. I'll share some of these strategies in the chapters ahead.

crisis

Nathan was an enthusiastic kindergarten student. But as a first-grader, when his parents went through a divorce, Nathan made little progress in school. He didn't learn to read or to do basic addition. He was too emotionally distraught. The climate in his home was so distracting, explosive, and unpredictable that he had no emotional security. Consequently, Nathan failed first grade and became a chronic behavior problem. It took two years of private tutoring and stabilizing of the home environment before Nathan was able to perform at the proper grade level.

When Leah was seven years old, her father died suddenly. She had been his favorite; he had rocked her and read to her, called her his "Sunshine," and taken her to the park every Saturday. After his death, Leah was despondent. She couldn't pay attention in class, and her reading skills lagged. She suffered greatly, and so did her schoolwork. She wasn't "psychologically available" to learn.

When Ryan's family relocated, he was in the middle of his sophomore year in high school. Always more interested in the social aspects of school, he was overwhelmed by the new environment and the fact that he didn't know anybody. His grades plummeted, and by the time he finished high school, he had lost any hope of ever attending college.

Are these kids' home and school situations rare? No, say learning specialists. In fact, in many children what seems to be a learning disability is often evidence of a much deeper problem: anxiety and turmoil underneath. We can send our kids to the best schools and even provide them with extra academic help, yet they can struggle in learning basic skills if there is constant stress at home.

"If there is turmoil in a child's heart or mind, it will cut learning by as much as 90 percent. Researchers all over the country are saying the same thing: There is a very high correlation between anxiety and the inability to learn," said Dr. Jordan.[7]

Being "emotionally available to learn" means kids can concentrate and focus on what the teacher is saying and on the printed words or math problems in their texts. But often, they are unable to do so because they can't turn off the inner conflict they bring with them to class. Children in the midst of a home torn by internal discord, divorce, or death manifest their feelings in several ways: sadness, aggression, acting out, extreme withdrawal, returning to bed-wetting, excessive crying and whining, failing grades, short attention span, daydreaming, headaches, or stomachaches. And the younger the child, the less likely it is that he can communicate his troubles with words.

As parents, how can we reestablish stability in times of crisis? There are ways we can support our kids in difficult family situations. If they have at least one caring adult to go through the experience with them and offer appropriate support, they can go through all kinds of adversity and emerge stronger and more capable of handling life.

During times of crisis, children need:

Affirmation that the parents, or remaining parent, will not leave them or quit loving them.

A *support system*, such as an aunt or grandparents who love and accept them. This can make all the difference in the world in their ability to cope with difficult times. Kids can surmount so many more problems if they have a network of support.

Reassurance that they *did not* cause the separation, death, or divorce. There needs to be honest, straight talk to relieve the children of guilt and feelings of being responsible for the crisis or problem, because kids tend to think that they are the cause for problems in their families.

Attentiveness to feelings and help putting the emotions they are feeling into words. Kids need to know that it is okay to feel hurt, be angry, or cry. If we as parents don't have time to listen and empathize, we must find someone who does.

Time for play and recreation. Exercise siphons excess nervous energy and stress and helps children to cope. And through a joint activity—throwing a ball or playing at the park together—they are more likely to open up and share what's going on inside.

Focused attention. The illness of a parent or grandparent, the arrival of a new brother or sister, parents' divorce, a move, changes and disappointments, for example, are more bearable for youngsters if they have extra bits of "I'm-all-here-for-you" time.

A *sense of order* reestablished in their lives. A stable, structured environment restores a sense of security to children in crisis. This structure should take the form of regular daily meals with conversation. Consistent hours for the children's sleeping and waking, studying, doing chores, and playing all contribute to a sense of security. When there are fairly consistent, reasonable family rules and guidelines, it helps reestablish stability.

Professional help, if the problem warrants it.[8] Our community has wonderful services and organizations, such as Calm Waters and The Kids Place, that provide support groups, art therapy, and programs designed to help children move through grief, loss, or family difficulties. Ask school counselors or psychologists if they know of such a facility in your area. You can also try the Internet, using key words like "children's grief support groups" or "grief centers" plus your city and state.

There are also some things to avoid doing if your children are exposed to a crisis situation or the family experiences trauma:

Don't deny or ignore the symptoms of depression or over-stress that you observe. Once when I was on a live talk show, a mother called in and said that her daughter Caroline had been a very good student until the fourth grade. Now in middle school, she had trouble in every subject, made poor grades, and hated school. I asked her, "What happened during your daughter's fourth-grade year? Any special problems or trauma in the family at that time?"

She went on to say that their oldest child, Caroline's sister, had died of leukemia following nine months of illness. It was apparent as she talked that although she had gotten help for her own grief, no one had helped Caroline with her profound sadness over the loss of her closest sibling. When Caroline seemed down or acted out as she did on occasion, she was told by family members to cheer up and not worry or upset her mother. Unfortunately, sometimes our own preoccupation with our family crisis can keep us from recognizing our children's struggles.

Following our conversation, Caroline's mom arranged for counseling for her daughter. In time, Caroline's overall attitude about school and life improved, she developed some new friendships, and she began to make progress in her studies.

Don't be demanding. Avoid communication that mainly consists of barking orders or applying pressure. When kids are acting in ways that are difficult for parents to deal with, much of the conversation becomes negative: "Straighten up. Don't do that. Stop whining."

Don't withdraw from your children; instead, be accessible, which often means getting help yourself to deal with your own issues so these emotions aren't played out through your children or dumped on them. Avoid being like those who get lost but refuse to ask for directions. Difficult times call for the help of friends, family, pastors, counselors, or others.

In Dr. Timothy Stuart's research, he found that people who had experienced significant levels of adversity in their lives but had succeeded all had at least one person in their lives who believed in them, encouraged them, and urged them to achieve beyond what they thought possible. Without a caring adult, children can be quickly overwhelmed by adversity. But "these two elements—adversity and a trusting relationship—interact with each other to create a fertile environment critical for a child's positive growth and development."[9]

As the family reestablishes stability and kids are helped to deal with the stress and changes brought on by a crisis situation, they can continue learning and growing without becoming overwhelmed or isolated. Whatever our family situation, one of the greatest things we can do for our children is to let them know we are committed to them for life: "I love you and will be here for you no matter what happens."

This commitment is particularly important to a child's sense of security in a time of crisis, such as a job change, a family move, or the death of a loved one. Also, in times of the child's *own* development crises—such as adolescence, transitioning between elementary school to middle school, or moving from middle school to high school—he needs to hear and know, "Whatever difficulties come our way, we are in this together, and we're going to make it!"

If the marriage has dissolved, commitment to the child is still an important stabilizing factor on the part of the parents. Children who have adjusted best are those who were free to love both parents and to develop affectionate relationships with stepparents.

stable and secure

All kids need a stable home base and the anchor of a strong sense of commitment in the family. Those foundations give them the peace of mind and inner security they need to grow. Then they are free to concentrate on reading, writing, and other studies in order to develop the building blocks to succeed in school and in life.

In some cases, school performance is maintained despite family instability. But in these cases, the children view the school arena as predictable and channel their energy toward schoolwork as a way of warding off or isolating their feelings about their family.

Teachers report that the most common classroom indicators of children experiencing disruption at home include: aggression toward peers, defiance of authority, moodiness, daydreaming, withdrawal, and declining grades. These kids may experience low self-worth, especially concerning their capacity to master new tasks and adapt to unfamiliar situations. Kids in turmoil also find it difficult to handle responsibility.[10]

Commitment, stability, and time together are some of the greatest gifts we can give our children. By doing so, we create the network of support they need to learn and succeed in school and life.

3

turning your preschooler
on to learning

Debbie— the mother of a bright, active four-year-old, Brian—
came to me in a quandary. "All Brian wants to do is watch television," she said. "His friend across the street moved, and now he
sits for hours in front of cartoons when he gets home from preschool. I have the baby to take care of, dinner to prepare, sewing,
laundry, and other chores to juggle, so I just can't entertain him
all the time. Yet I want him to be ready for kindergarten. What
can I do?"

One of the most critical times of intellectual development is
the first five years. During this time, the foundation is being laid
for all later skills: reading, writing, reasoning, math, and communication. Brain research shows that the experiences a child
has during the early years affect the wiring and connections of
the brain. Yet kids of all ages are learning all the time, throughout childhood to adolescence. No matter what age your kids are,
it's "better late than never" to get involved in their learning.

Most young children spend an enormous amount of time in
front of a screen watching television, playing video games, or on
the computer—about three times longer than they spend reading

3

or being read to. Nearly two-thirds of kids under age two spend a couple of hours a day viewing TV even though the American Academy of Pediatrics has recommended that kids under two not watch television at all because it's such a critical period for young children's intellectual, social, and physical development.[1]

What's the problem with media overload? Prolonged television viewing is a passive pastime that stifles children's creativity, shortens their attention span, stunts their language ability, deprives them of conversation and questioning, and decreases physical activity.[2] A recent study shows that children with a television in their bedroom or who live in households where the TV is on most or all of the time are less likely to be able to read by age six than children who have less access to a TV.[3]

In addition, psychologists report that young children are experiencing tremendous stress from the visual overload of too much television viewing, including such damage as inner-ear problems, nearsightedness, and increased aggressive behavior. Like Brian's mom, you may be very busy keeping up with your job, doing housework, carpooling, and caring for your child's siblings. He may be in preschool or a Mother's Day Out program part of the week, but during his hours at home, how can you encourage your child to discover the joy of learning, develop readiness skills in a low-stress atmosphere, and meet his needs developmentally? The following activities benefit preschool and elementary-age kids and can be done with a parent, grandparent, or older sibling.

pretend play

Pretend play is a vital part of children's learning processes, not a waste of time. It encourages the development of language, vocabulary, and communication skills; helps children learn to deal with fears and difficult situations; and develops creativity. As kids think, plan, and carry out an idea, they are building confidence in solving problems.

One of the best ways to encourage imaginative play is to allow our preschoolers enough time to play in an unhurried atmosphere and provide costumes, props, and toys that stimulate pretend play. Here are some suggestions:[4]

- Dress-up clothes, long garments, old costume jewelry and accessories, vests, ties (your local thrift store is a great place to find these inexpensively)

- Hats of many shapes and sizes—fireman's hat, straw hat, cowboy hat, glamorous hat, baseball cap, grandfather's hat

- Medical kits, props for playing "hospital," Acc bandages

- Travel props—tickets, tourist guidebook, small suitcase, purse, old camera, play money

- Office props—old or play telephone, adding machine, receipt book, old typewriter or computer

- Puppets—homemade or bought, materials to make a backdrop, box to make a stage

Along with these pretend-play resources, include pencils and paper to motivate your kids to learn to read and write (more about this in a later chapter). Then add some space where they can spread out and create their own play. Last, we need to give our preschoolers enough time to engage in pretend play. When they are overscheduled with so many outside activities—wonderful activities such as music classes, gymnastics, soccer, preschool, and church activities—they don't have time to initiate imaginative play.

Providing them time and space gives kids permission to play. Children who are made to feel guilty about "wasting time" or "messing up the house" with their pretend play don't develop the initiative to pretend. Also, as you observe their play, you can see what your kids are thinking about and talking about. This provides valuable insight into their interests, gifts, and personalities.

art fosters your child's development

Kids who are encouraged to express themselves through art develop creative-thinking skills they can use to problem-solve as they grow. Their large-motor and fine-motor skills improve as they work with clay, draw with crayons, finger paint, or use scissors.

All it takes to foster artistic development is having some art materials at home and encouraging your child to use them. A great way to make these materials accessible to your child is to make your own "Amazing Art Box" in a plastic container. A cabinet by the kitchen table is a good place to keep it. Be sure to include a plastic place mat for him to put down in case he spills and an apron or Dad's old T-shirt to protect his clothing.

Pencils and paper are inexpensive basics for your art box. The best readers, writers, and artists of today were "pencil-and-paper kids" who spent a lot of their preschool years scribbling and drawing at home.[5]

You could also include some of the following materials in the art box: large washable crayons, washable markers, finger paints, safety scissors, a glue stick, bright catalogs and magazines, colored construction paper and paper plates, stickers (cats, clowns, cars, trucks, balloons), scraps of fabric, pom-poms, glitter glue, pipe cleaners, stamp pads, yarn, bright-colored tissue paper and wallpaper, strings, buttons, and different colors of clay (homemade or purchased).

Several times a week you might suggest that your child get out the art box and make something. Let your child's interests lead. If she currently is fascinated with cats, lead in that direction. If firemen and fire trucks capture his interest at present, ask him to draw a picture of a brave rescue. Or say, "It's art time. Let's get out some construction paper and stickers and make a get-well card for Grandma."

Art time can be as varied as your child's imagination. One day it might consist of listening to a story on cassette and illustrating the story. Another day, pretend food can be made out of clay for the child's dolls to "eat" at a tea party.

Display your child's creations on the refrigerator door, on

the family bulletin board, or in a frame. Take the time to show an active interest in your child's artistic efforts and creations by making comments or asking questions: "How did you mix that red and blue together so smoothly in the rainbow?" "I like the way you drew the grass in short, choppy strokes."

When our son Chris, at five years old, used a ruler and various colored pencils to create a picture of the "Steadfast Tin Soldier" we'd just read about in a children's story, we framed his work of art and hung it in the living room. His aunts liked it so much that they asked him to draw a Steadfast Tin Soldier for them to display in their homes. What an encouragement to Chris's budding interest in art!

Every child is creative in some way or another, and giving your child resources, space, time, and encouragement to develop his artistic ability will yield wonderful results in his development.

bars, balls, and balance

Preschoolers are like little Energizer bunnies. With more energy than we can imagine, they need resources to channel all that energy and to develop physically. Large-muscle exercisers—both inside and outside the home—can be simple, inexpensive, and fun. Our preschooler loved his small Nerf basketball and hoop, which fit on a door and gave him something to do with his boundless energy on rainy days, and he used it through his teen years. If it seems your preschooler is always getting into trouble, it may be that he doesn't have enough accessible ways to expend energy. Make sure you have some of the following equipment available around your home and yard:

- Playground equipment for climbing, swinging, and playing

- Balance beam (which you can make yourself with cement blocks and a sturdy board)

- Riding toys

- Horseshoes, beanbags, pounding toys, balls of all sizes

- Rebounder (a small indoor trampoline; kids can jump to their favorite music)

Shape sorters, puzzles, Legos, blocks, and construction toys are all good small-muscle toys. Blocks are the ideal toy and contribute to almost every aspect of a child's learning, especially math.

someone's in the kitchen with mom

With a little ingenuity and lots of patience on your part, cooking provides opportunities for a preschooler to learn math and weight-volume concepts and to engage in simple science experiments in the kitchen. Teach your child to follow a simple recipe. She can make her own pudding with a little help from you. You read the recipe step-by-step, and your child measures, stirs, and, of course, licks the bowl. Along the way, talk about what you are doing.

While you are preparing meals, let your child set the table or string together different colors of macaroni. This exercise helps develop muscle and hand-eye coordination. As you prepare a dish, ask your child, "What does this smell like? What do you think it will taste like?" Let her count cookies as she puts them on the plate for you. As you allow your child to help you measure, she begins to understand weight-volume concepts.

who's afraid of the big bad wolf?

Before bedtime, read a story to your child, and before the end of the story, stop and ask, "What do you think might happen now?" Active reading and listening will bring your child countless benefits later in the form of improved comprehension skills and the desire to read. Give preschoolers wordless picture books they can "read" to relax before naptime. These creative books tell a well-developed story in pictures while enriching your child's language and imagination skills.

"Kindergarten children who know a lot about written language usually have parents who believe that reading is important and who seize every opportunity to act on that conviction by reading to their children," say reading experts.[6] In the chapter on reading, chapter 4, you'll find more ideas for fostering your child's reading skills as she grows. In addition, *The Read-Aloud Handbook*[7] and *Honey for a Child's Heart*[8] list hundreds of great books to select from.

conversing with preschoolers

Once, I was sitting in our local library doing research, and a mother and two children came in the door. As the mom talked with the librarian, her little girl, about three or four years of age, listened. During a pause in the adults' conversation, she looked up eagerly and said, "Did you know I got a bike for my birthday?" Several times she posed her question, but no one was listening.

A few minutes later she said, "My cat ran away; I miss my kitty," but still no response. Finally the preschooler turned and wandered away.

Often, we tell our preschool children not to interrupt us, but the truth is that many times they can't get a word in edgewise. I'll admit it's hard to listen to the fourth telling of a long, long story your three-year-old relates, but most of us parents do more talking than listening. There's a story of a mom whose son got home from kindergarten and tried to tell her what had happened on the playground that day. She was bustling around the kitchen saying, "I'm listening, I'm listening," but her mind was far away. Finally, her son got her to get down on his level; he put his little hands around her face and said, "But Mommy, would you listen with your face?"

Engaging in conversations with preschoolers is a great investment in their language skills. Talk and listen; ask questions and be open to theirs. It stimulates our children's interest in the world around them when we answer their seemingly endless questions: "Why is the moon round?" "Why is my hair red?" "Where does bread come from?"

recording fun

A recorder can be one of the best friends a busy mother ever had. Here are some ways to use the recorder to enhance your child's learning:

- Your preschooler can recite stories into a cassette or video recorder—perhaps his latest made-up story or his own rendition of "The Three Bears."

- If your child is away from you for a day or a weekend at her grandparents' house, she can take along her own tape recorder and at naptime listen to a story you have prerecorded. The auditory stimulation is great, and hearing your voice is reassuring.

- CDs and tapes are great outlets for the energetic preschooler. You can take the music along on errands or trips and let your child listen and sing along as he rides in the car.

- Many stories and books for children are available on tape or CD. Your child can also listen to a story in the kitchen while you cook dinner or to help her wind down at naptime.

love notes

Even before he can read, receiving notes you have written to him gets your child interested in the written word. As you combine easy words he can recognize with pictures, you create a message perfect for the prereader to figure out. "I (picture of a heart) you!" written on a sticky note on the bathroom mirror can brighten up his day. Or "Let's go to the (picture of park or tree) today." Simultaneously, his curiosity about language is stimulated and he is reminded of your love. As your child grows, he might begin to surprise you with little notes of his own, such as the one I received years ago from my son Chris:

MOM—I LOVE miy mom and miy mom love me.
LOVE Chris

Chris is now thirty years old and serving on the other side of the world in the military, but I still treasure the note. Your child can put reminders on the bulletin board or dictate a thank-you note to Grandma or Grandpa for a birthday present. Later, writing will come more naturally for your child and he will enjoy writing because of these early opportunities provided at home.

When your child does try to sound out words, it's okay to accept the "invented spelling" he uses rather than discouraging him by criticizing his less-than-perfect efforts. As your child's reading vocabulary develops through elementary school, his spelling vocabulary will also expand.

our walks with two-year-olds

Walks arc a terrific way to open your preschooler's eyes to the world around her and provide unlimited resources for learning.

It's also a great way to spend time with your child. Splash in puddles after it rains or take a stargazing walk at night. Even a simple walk around the block can become a learning adventure. We enjoyed doing things such as these:

- Sticky-tape walks: Place masking tape around your child's wrists with the sticky side out. In autumn, look for signs of fall and put those on the tape. When you get home, make a collage of what you have found.

- Smelly walks: Smell as you go and determine what you are smelling.

- Color walks: Find all red things on your walk. The next day, find all the yellow things around your block, and so on.[9]

- "I Spy" walks: Take turns "spying" something and letting the other person guess it.

- "How many?" walks: Start your walk by asking, "How many different kinds of flowers [or leaves, rocks, butterflies—whatever is in your neighborhood] can we find today?"

time well spent

These activities with our kids take some time, but it is time well spent. The thirty minutes you spend with your child investigating a spider spinning a web plant valuable seeds as he asks questions and you share what you know. Maybe later he'll draw a picture of a spider, or you can get a book about spiders from the library. As you follow the leading of your child's interest and your own intuition, this time might be more valuable in helping your child become a lifelong learner than a whole day in an ordinary school setting.

Enjoy the precious, fleeting preschool years with your child, and allow him to unhurriedly enjoy this time too. One mother asked me, "But will my child be learning what he is supposed to and be prepared for kindergarten? Should I be doing workbooks with him? I'm not sure I'm doing the right things at home."

If you're giving your child resources to play and learn, adding your own creative ideas, talking and listening, encouraging him in his efforts and interests, then a whole world of discovery and wonder will be open to him. You'll be laying a good foundation for school skills. And most of all, you can be confident that he'll become a lifelong learner, ready for all of the challenges that lie ahead.

raising readers

Susan was concerned that her kids were rarely assigned the classics in school. So when they were young, she started them on Beatrix Potter and A. A. Milne. Later she found if she wanted them to read books such as *Little Women, Tom Sawyer, Ivanhoe, The Scarlet Letter,* or *Moby-Dick,* she'd have to introduce them to these books as well. So their home reading plan evolved, which included books she assigned her kids to read in addition to their regular schoolwork. "No one else in my class has to read these books!" her daughters occasionally complained. But Susan stuck with the plan, continued reading aloud a few times a week as a family, and encouraged her children's independent reading as well.

Some years later, she got a thank-you letter from her oldest daughter. Ann had just found out she was exempt from a whole year of college freshman English because of acing an advanced placement test in English literature. Out of thirty students who took the test, only two were able to complete it, and Ann earned the only 5 (on a scale of 1-5, with 5 being the highest). She knew it was all the reading she'd done at home that had made the difference. Her younger sister and brother are reading the same books. Her brother Josh has multiple handicaps but has still become an avid reader. Their secret? Reading classics, memorizing poetry, limiting TV, and developing a family library.

how to produce children with reading disabilities

Let's look at the opposite kind of home environment. "I see a real pattern among children with reading disabilities," noted Karen Gale, a reading specialist, about her work tutoring children and adults in reading. Her experience led us to the following step-by-step recipe for producing poor reading skills in children:

1. Make sure you, the parent, are very busy and have little time for your children.
2. Don't read very much yourself.
3. Read aloud to your children infrequently or not at all.
4. Maintain an entertainment-oriented home, with television, videos, and movies receiving top priority.
5. Provide your children with nonstop access to Nintendo Game Boys, computer games, and the Internet.

Karen has observed this pattern over and over again in her years of teaching hundreds of children and adults to read. She's convinced that poor reading skills are rarely due to a disability in the individual but rather to a home environment similar to the above formula.

why is reading so important?

Learning specialists say that reading is the most important of all study skills. This is true not just for English class but also for history, science, and math (especially in understanding math concepts and word problems). In fact, the majority of all school-work requires reading. After the third grade, all school subjects require language skills in some way. Spelling and grammar abilities are directly related to reading experiences, and listening skills are a by-product of being read to. Critical thinking and imagination flow out of reading time. Good writing and speaking abilities are a result of the amount and quality of reading. Vocabulary development is enhanced by reading; in fact, business leaders point to the relationship of high vocabulary to success in *any* field.

So it is critical that children become good readers, because their reading level will significantly impact their success or failure at school. Reading is a door to learning, and our efforts should be aimed toward the goal of producing motivated, lifelong readers.

home life is the key

It is a great thing to start life with a small number of really good books which are your very own.

—SIR ARTHUR CONAN DOYLE

Most schools these days are highly focused on reading. Every school and library seems to have an incentive program designed to get kids to read books. These programs are great, but research shows that in spite of concerted efforts to increase reading achievement in the elementary grades, relatively few gains in this area have been evidenced on the national assessments compared to previous years.[1] What researchers are finding is that instead of pizza contests and free amusement park tickets to reward reading, good readers are produced by parents who place limits on television viewing, emphasize homework completion, and encourage reading by having an abundance of interesting materials available.

In other research, a quarter of a million American students from ages nine through seventeen were studied. It was concluded that it is the child's *home* that makes the greatest difference in his reading ability, not his IQ or the type of innovative reading program used at his school.[2]

I loved the summer reading programs at our local library and the special things my kids' teachers did to encourage reading. I think it's great that millions of dollars are being spent each year in an attempt to teach our children to learn to read at school. We need to invest in our children's education! Yet this tremendous spending is in vain if our kids don't get the practice necessary to become fluent readers. Just as an athlete's physical muscles must be exercised persistently if he is to develop strength for the game, students' reading "muscles" need to be exercised at home. Kids need to continue to develop speed and comprehension skills so that when a challenging book such as Emily Brontë's *Wuthering Heights* or Shakespeare's *Hamlet* is assigned in high school, they will be able to read, understand, and respond to it.

Beyond that, we want our children to read not just because

Make an alphabet book for your child. Put a diffcrent letter and photo of something that your child loves or connects with on each page. For example, the "D" page could feature a photo of your child with her dog, the "G" page a picture of her grandparents, and the "S" page her favorite sport. There are also many cute alphabet board-books available for toddlers and preschoolers.

making the most of the way kids learn

Because one of the major learning methods of children is imitation, your role modeling can instill a love of reading in your children. If you don't like to read, try to find *something* you would like to know more about. Then take time and read about it. Please don't tell your children, "It's okay if you're not good in reading; I wasn't." Poor ding is not a disease your children can catch, but parents do to pass along their habits and attitudes concerning reading. you're a couch potato in front of the TV every evening, your ill probably become couch potatoes too. But if they see ed up with a good book after dinner or before bedtime, if ou laugh at a comic or discuss an editorial in a news- e reading, they'll see that you don't just tell them to lso practice it. And they'll likely welcome reading as of their own lifestyles.

h the heart with one book, it can transform

—ALLAN BLOOM

they have to but because they want to. Developing a love for reading will provide them a lifetime of enjoyment.

encouraging the preschooler and elementary reader

Long before babies understand spoken language, their early en-counters with words, stories, books, singing, talking, and reading provide the stimulation their brains need. Research shows that books read aloud to kids provide a significantly larger range of words than listening to TV or conversation—and the size of a preschooler's vocabulary is a strong predictor of her success as a reader.[3] In a~ tion to the ideas provided in chapter 3, here are some simple~ you can do to promote reading in your young child's life:

Place a label on her toy box, closet, drawers. *possessions.* Put your child's name on her bedr~ her that words have meaning and can be u~ belongings.

Read Mother Goose nursery rhyme *and rhyming books (such as Dr. S* exposed to lots of poetry prepare~ phonics (the decoding of word~ their own poetry.

Help her read words *or on the road.* Some ness signs, recipe~ alphabet letters o~ try to read.

reading resources

Provide a variety of reading resources at home that fit with each of your kids' particular areas of interest. Every child has something he's interested in. I am constantly amazed at how different and unique each child's reading interests are, and I'm convinced that if we look hard enough, we can find something each one will enjoy reading about.

Our oldest son, Justin, liked compelling fiction, mysteries, war stories, and history. In contrast, our son Chris wanted to read for facts; he liked reading encyclopedias, information about the rainfall of Nebraska, and statistics on NFL football teams. He devoured the sports page of the daily newspaper and loved biographies of sports heroes. Alison liked reading about art, gymnastics, and ballet. She loved biographies of famous women such as Helen Keller, Harriet Tubman, and Clara Barton.

The library was a terrific resource for discovering these individual interests. Every two weeks, we trekked to the library to stock up on reading material and give each child an ever-changing supply of books. Given time to browse, the children always found books I never would have thought of.

When we came home, I found visible, accessible places to put the books—in a big basket by our easy chair, in a neat stack on the coffee table, on a shelf by the children's beds, and in the car on trips. For youngsters, what is out of sight is truly out of mind, so books need to be in a highly visible spot (and the TV behind the closed doors of a cabinet).

build a home library

Develop your own personal library at home with books and materials for different ages, stages, and interests. It doesn't have to cost a lot to build a family library. Many excellent children's books and classics are available in paperback at reasonable prices. You can also get books inexpensively at used-book sales and book fairs held by schools and libraries. Many parents stock up on books from thrift stores and garage sales, where books are often fifty cents each or less. One of our best investments was a good set of encyclopedias—a great thing to have on the shelf to lessen your children's dependence on the Internet. An atlas is very helpful, and you probably want to stock your shelves with children's classics and a set of fairy tales long before they're ready to read them.

Giving your kids books as gifts on special occasions and birthdays sends a powerful message to them that books are valuable! Tell grandparents you're building a home library and let them know what types of books your kids like. Make books part of your Christmas and holiday traditions. Each year, I bought a new Christmas book for our kids, and during the holidays, these special books sat in a big basket with a bright bow by the fireplace for us to read together. The books still remain there, and now our kids come in and read them to *their* children. Each year, I give a new Christmas book to our children's families so they can build their home libraries.

Commemorate milestones in your kids' lives with a new book. You might consider inscribing it. Some examples are: "To Caitlin, on her first day of kindergarten. Love, Nandy." "For Noah, with love and hugs for your graduation from middle school!" A gift certificate to a bookstore with a special children's section is a great gift. So is a membership in a book club suited to your children's ages and interests. Your children could start their own after-school book club in the neighborhood and discuss one book a month.

Don't stop with books. Magazines offer great reading motivation for kids of all ages, and they're available on specialized topics such as sports, nature, science, history, crafts, skateboarding, and just about every area of interest imaginable. I do recommend you preview any magazine choices, as some magazines marketed at children and teenagers contain quite inappropriate material.

preview the reading material

Evaluate questionable books—either part of your children's reading curriculum at school or merely one that they have chosen themselves—to determine if they are appropriate for your family and for your kids' maturity. Don't take the opinions of others as the last word. See what values and beliefs you feel the books promote and how they line up with what you want your children to be learning. If you don't object to a certain book but are somewhat concerned about violent battle scenes or frightening parts of the story, read them along with your children and use them as a springboard to good discussions.

One example of controversial books is the HARRY POTTER series, which has gotten thousands of kids "hooked on books" and excited about reading but are a cause of concern to many parents who find the occult references and wizardry objectionable. Surely they are imaginative and compelling reading, but even some parents and teachers who approved of the first two or three books find the content of books four and five darker or inappropriate for their children.

I encourage you to read the HARRY POTTER books yourself before introducing them to your kids or before you complain when a teacher has assigned them. (Note: I am not promoting nor denouncing the reading of the HARRY POTTER books.) You can also go to www.pluggedinonline.com for book reviews, helpful information for parents, and updates on new developments in Harry Potter's world.

read-aloud time at home

Reading aloud has lots of benefits for young readers. When you tell stories or read aloud from books without pictures, kids have to *imagine* the pictures, whereas with television, video, and computer, they are depending on someone else's made-up pictures. Hearing good literature read aloud provides children a rich and colorful model for their language development and enlarges their vocabulary. It lengthens their attention span and helps them learn to follow directions better. Not surprisingly, teachers report that a steady diet of good literature read aloud at home also improves students' attitudes toward school.

Start reading aloud to your kids at a very early age. Your three- or six-month-old baby might not understand the words to Margaret Wise Brown's *Goodnight Moon* or Dr. Seuss's *Green Eggs and Ham,* but hearing you read the words aloud will help her associate reading with something warm and pleasurable.

In the fall and winter when dark came early and the cold wind blew outside, our school-age children loved snuggling up by the fireplace in sleeping bags and listening while Dad read one chapter a night of a favorite series. Laura Ingalls Wilder's LITTLE HOUSE books and C. S. Lewis's THE CHRONICLES OF NARNIA were all-time favorites. Kids love chapter and series books because a sense of anticipation builds about what the next episode or book is going to hold. Once a child has enjoyed one of the author's books, she wants to read the rest in the series.

These days, there are more series books than ever available for kids of all ages. Even kindergarteners and first-graders can begin to enjoy chapter books (as opposed to picture books), such as the JUNIE B. JONES books, the MAGIC TREE HOUSE series, the BOXCAR CHILDREN books, and books by E. B. White. Older children love C. S. Lewis's THE CHRONICLES OF NARNIA series, the historical AMERICAN DIARY series, the AMERICAN GIRLS series, NANCY DREW and THE HARDY BOYS mysteries, and many others. Bookstores and libraries have special sections devoted to series books, so they're easy to find.

when can you find the time?

As a busy parent, when can you find the time to read aloud to your children? Even if you don't have large blocks of time to devote to reading, you can seize random moments throughout the day.

For example, when you're waiting at the pediatrician or dentist with your kids, take along a couple of books to read aloud. You can read to your children almost anywhere. Take along a book and read at the park or the beach. Let your kids listen to books on tape or CD at bedtime to help them wind down.

For one family I know, the favorite read-aloud place is the kitchen. Dad has to be away some evenings, but when he's home, he always does the dishes after dinner so the children can pull up chairs around Mom, who sits at the table and reads aloud to the whole family.

Wherever and whenever you do it, reading together fosters family closeness and bonding. Time spent reading to your children at bedtime produces benefits for the relationship, whatever the age. Reading aloud is equally important for older children. Don't stop reading to them just because they've learned how! Even after kids are proficient readers, they need to keep hearing books read aloud. After a time, reading aloud as a family becomes a habit nobody wants to give up. Besides meeting their personal needs, it helps kids continue enjoying books for entertainment so they won't automatically associate reading with workbooks, drills, and tests.

independent reading

Having time to read silently is also important for your children's development because independent reading increases reading speed, comprehension, and vocabulary. Giving fifteen or twenty extra minutes of lights-on time at bedtime for kids to read can inspire their interest in books. It also helps to establish some quiet times and places at home for reading. For example, you could put a sheet over a table and add a few pillows.

You might want to have silent reading time each week, in which all of you get comfy in the family room and read independently. Periodically, take a few minutes to discuss what each person has been reading.

kicking the TV habit

Just as reading aloud multiplies a child's learning, a steady diet of television nullifies it. Each family is different, but we can all develop some strategies for dealing with the TV and make a conscious effort to reduce the part it plays in our family lifestyle. Why? Besides the effects listed in chapter 3, the low quality of morals and high degree of violence portrayed on many shows is destructive to your child's developing character. During viewing times, kids generally aren't interacting with others, reading, playing, talking, or helping anyone.

Further, television watching stunts the imagination.[4] Students who can't picture the characters and action from the written word (because they've done little reading) are handicapped when they have more lengthy, advanced reading without illustrations. Because too much television viewing handicaps learning, what can we do to limit it? The best way is to provide appealing alternatives, such as family projects, board games, sports, art, and outdoor activities.

Another way to reduce the impact of TV is to have the school week be a "no TV zone." You can limit TV viewing to the weekend and then watch only in moderation. Some families allow their children to record their favorite shows during the week and watch them on the weekend.

For many families, the most difficult part of limiting kids' television viewing is the example set by parents. Sometimes we have to take a long, hard look at our own habits and make some initially painful decisions for the best interests of our children. Do we often have the television on in the background, even when we're not really watching it? Do we turn the set on every night after dinner just out of habit? Is the TV the largest piece of furniture in the family room? We each need to make an assessment of how much importance we're placing on the television as compared to other family and individual activities. Taking even one step in the direction of decreasing screen time can quickly produce noticeable results, and if you combine that with other strategies for encouraging reading, you'll be well on your way to raising a lifelong bookworm.

raising writers

*Children's ability to talk, listen, read, and write will
have a lifelong effect on their ability to learn. In turn,
parents have a profound influence on the development
of these skills during the preschool years and beyond.*

—DONALD GRAVES AND VIRGINIA STUART, *WRITE FROM THE START*[1]

Writing isn't just another subject taught in school. There is
a strong relationship between writing and thinking, so kids who
become good writers are more successful in every subject. They
excel in self-expression, become more self-reliant, and enjoy
learning more—from first grade all the way through college and
beyond. Kids who write at home become better writers overall.

As parents, we tend to encourage our kids to develop in the
areas in which we're interested. If you love sports, for example,
you probably put a ball in your baby's hands and taught him
how to bounce, handle, and later kick it. You may have signed
your four-year-old up for a peewee soccer team. If you're an
artist, you probably have a table in your house with paint, clay,
and other art supplies for your kids to use. A physicist I know
helped his nine-year-old son build a model of a working dam just
because they'd seen a picture in a book and his son wanted to

try it. When that kind of influence happens, as long as we don't push or force the activity, our child more than likely develops an aptitude or interest in the sport or hobby.

Because I'd written letters and poems all my life (even before writing professionally), my kids were surrounded by words. I left lists for them if I had to be away for the afternoon: chores to be done, fun activities, and a few don'ts. Besides leaving notes of encouragement on yellow sticky notes, I put messages in their lunch boxes, wrote them poems on special occasions, and involved them in generating ideas for our family Christmas letter.

When they began their own writing, I saved each of their stories and poems in a file folder after displaying them on the bulletin board. The result? Although our kids are very different from each other in aptitude, each became a competent writer. Justin majored in English and uses writing in many phases of his career, Chris was a premed student whose writing skills enabled him to excel in humanities and language courses in addition to the science courses he took in college, and Alison is an extremely creative writer who has written songs and poems (some that have been published).

You don't have to be a professional writer to encourage your kids' writing skills. In this chapter, you'll find many easy ways to become a writing family.

stages of writing skills development

First, it helps to understand the way writing skills develop. Although children mature according to their own schedule, we know that when given the time, encouragement, and materials to write, normal students will progress through the following developmental stages:

Preschool: Basic language patterns are forming, and the children are constantly building vocabulary. Drawing and scribbling are important prewriting activities that develop expression, coordination, and fine-motor skills. The children can dictate stories orally while someone writes them down.

Kindergarten and first grade: Kids in this age group tend to write in the same way they play blocks or other games—for the sake of the activity rather than for the final product. They rehearse by drawing and talking. They sometimes use invented spelling (in which letter names represent sounds), and can often produce delightful poems, plays, and stories.

Second and third grades: At this age, children usually become more fluent writers. Because of an increasing sense of audience and a desire to get things right, they begin to move toward more conventional spelling and editing by grade three. They can write letters as well as stories with a plot, sequence, and dialogue.

Grades four through six: Vocabulary continues to build so that by fifth grade, children can usually correctly spell most of the words used in their writing. They learn to revise for better meaning and mechanics. They can write stories several pages long with conflict, characterization, and dialogue. They learn to take notes, write factual stories, and use reference materials such as a dictionary and thesaurus.

Grades seven through nine: Typical junior high school writers organize and compose essays, stories, and reports. Writing flows more easily, the students' vocabulary is wider, and they are more descriptive. Editing and revising their first draft into a polished final copy will hopefully become a normal part of their writing process.

Grades ten through twelve: High school students gain practice in writing well-organized expository papers, descriptive essays, and narrative essays. They learn to write a research paper using library resources. In the process, they take notes, form outlines, add footnotes, and make a bibliography. By the end of high school, their writing skills should be solid and competent.

the missing link

School writing programs have received increasing attention over the past few decades. Schools have made efforts to increase the frequency of writing assignments, and many require that students "write across the curriculum" (that is, write in all subjects, not just in English class). Thousands of teachers have had instruction in how to teach writing effectively. Yet the findings of national education progress reports show that the most important and the most absent ingredient in writing skill development is the home environment.

One study, by Dr. Judy Abbott at West Virginia University, was conducted with a group of fifth-grade students termed "avid writers" who chose to write on their own and were skillful language users who had more interest in writing than their peers did. Through hundreds of hours of observation and interviews in the kids' homes, Dr. Abbott identified these factors in their family lives that supported their interest in writing:[2]

The kids had lots of interaction with adults. Being surrounded by conversation at home helped immensely when they began to take on the challenges of written language through reading and writing.

Their first writing attempts were encouraged. Parents treated their first writing attempts as real writing and took it seriously. They tried to decipher what had been written and even had the child read it to them. The children weren't told, "Oh, you're just doing pretend writing. I can't read that." Even when using invented spelling, their early writings were treated as real language.

They had at least one adult who was instrumental in interacting with them and their writing. Their mom or a certain teacher took time to read aloud to them, talk with them about school issues, and encourage their written expression with statements such as, "That's such a good story you just told me. Why don't you write it down?" or "Can I see what you've been writing?" They suggested things to write, such as a list of friends to invite to a party or a get-well card to someone.

Parents provided time and resources for them to write. One mom gave her son a journal and told him that if he had trouble falling asleep, he could write down his thoughts. Parents of the young writers also provided writing items, such as pens, paper, markers, and computer access.

This study underscores how important adults are in facilitating a child's interest and developing skill in writing. And in the examples given, what the parents supplied didn't take lots of money or special classes.

Your children also can become fluent, lifelong writers when you provide them four basic keys at home: role models, resources, reasons, and encouragement.

teach by example

Mary sat at the kitchen table, writing her weekly grocery list and figuring her checkbook balance. She addressed an envelope to mail a birthday card to her sister in Iowa. Five-year-old Abby sat quietly next to her mother, busy with her own "writing" projects. In invented spelling she wrote a list of food for her doll's birthday party and drew pictures of what her dolls needed on Christmas.

Just as we help our children by showing them how to make a bed, set the table, throw a baseball, or ride a bicycle, we can show them how to write by writing as we go about our ordinary business at home.

Parents who write (and let their kids see them doing so) demonstrate that writing has value. Their children see that writing is a normal, worthwhile way to spend time. When our children observe us at the computer writing a letter to the editor of the local newspaper or to our congressperson about an important issue, they see that writing serves a useful purpose in our everyday lives.

At the same time, we parents show our children the process we go through to produce that writing—making a mistake, sometimes crossing out lines, correcting words, or even deleting an entire document and starting again. They begin to realize that writing is a process, something they don't have to get right the first time they try. When we discuss a newspaper article or read a letter aloud and ask, "How does this sound?" our kids are shown that reading and writing are meant to be shared.

So the next time you're jotting down a few words in a birthday card, writing a thank-you note, or filling out boring insurance forms, don't hide at your bedroom desk. Let your child see you writing. Depending on his age, he can write his own note, draw, or make a list of his favorite stuffed animals or jobs he needs to do.

When you make a shopping list, give your child an opportunity to make her own list. She can then see that writing is a part of everyday life. Research has proven that this "writing alongside" works much better than trying to teach a child to write by requiring her to do exercises in a workbook.

When our kids were young, I wrote Valentine's Day poems for them and my husband and read them at breakfast or dinner. Sometimes I wrote just for fun or to express my affection. I posted inspiring or humorous quotes on the refrigerator. They sometimes saw me writing in a journal or jotting a note to an out-of-town friend, so they grew up thinking of writing as a regular part of life, not just as something they had to do at school. And as a result, their attitudes toward school writing were generally positive and reflected an "I can do it" feeling. They figured if Mom could do it, so could they.

love notes in lunch boxes

To help your kids realize that letter writing can be fun, write them notes and put them in their lunch boxes, on their pillows, on their mirrors, or in the camp suitcase. Soon you will probably begin getting messages back.

Even if the children are too young to read very well, they will try to work out what the message says. "It amazes me how they can figure out a note if it's something Mother wrote: 'I love you'; 'Have a good day!'" said one teacher. These are simple things, but they're essential in giving children the motivation to write.

Leave practical messages on their bathroom mirror such as, "Don't forget to clean your room," and encouraging words such as, "Good luck on your science test!" In the course of our normal, everyday routines, we have a unique opportunity to foster this "writing as lifestyle" attitude as we model writing as a natural, useful, and enjoyable activity.

resources for writing

If our kids are going to write at home, they need resources. And, as I have already noted in the last chapter, the most vital resource is reading. A diversity of reading materials and opportunities at home encourages our kids to write. When they hear good literature read aloud, it expands their store of words and meanings, sharpens their perception of correct phrasing, introduces different writing styles, and increases comprehension and thinking skills.

Frequent conversation is another vital language resource. During conversations with parents and siblings, kids learn to give reasons for their opinions, discuss alternatives to problems, express their feelings, and think more clearly. Good thinkers tend to be good writers. Conversing with our children about the world around them gives them a great foundation for the development of writing skills.

We can ask our children to describe an event or person from their day. We can encourage their observations and feelings. It helps if we build time for sharing ideas into our daily routine. For some families, around the dinner table in the evening works best, even if it's at McDonald's or a local restaurant. For others, it's at breakfast or bedtime. Some of the best conversations are stirred up during a walk around the block or while our kids are working alongside us raking leaves, doing dishes, or cooking.

Ask simple questions such as, "What's the most interesting thing you did, learned, or saw today?" "What are you thankful for?" or "What's your biggest pet peeve?" Ask your kids to share about something they've been reading or learning. Then provide accessible materials for drawing: crayons, colored pencils, writing pencils, paper for drawing, a blackboard and chalk, felt-tip pens, and paint. Most early readers and good writers had access to writing materials at home and did lots of drawing. As relayed in *What Works: Research About Teaching and Learning*, "Studies of very young children show that their carefully formed scrawls have meaning to them and that this writing actually helps them develop language skills."[3] Even before they are old enough to read and write, toddlers like to draw and scribble messages.

Plastic or metal letters on a felt or magnetic board or the refrigerator are useful for preschoolers' early writing attempts. Some young children like to write using computer keyboards;

others like to dictate stories to Mom or Dad, who write them down and read them back. Dictating a story into a cassette or video recorder is also fun for some children.

dramatic play

Dramatic or pretend play motivates children to want to learn to read and write. As I shared in chapter 3, if we put pencils and paper near their other toys, kids start to write as a part of their play. For example, when they play "office," they can write letters, address them, and then "mail" them in their own make-believe mailbox. Sometimes children like to make labels for their toys and signs for their rooms: "SaraJane Bear"; "Keep out!"; "Girls only!"

Freeda, a creative writing teacher I know, found that the favorite pretend play of her daughter Laura was "store." With a receipt book from an office store, an old adding machine, and a telephone mounted on the wall, the "store" generated many hours of creative play and writing orders, receipts, lists of returned merchandise, and other "business" records.

For several years, my daughter, Alison, enjoyed playing "hospital" and making short medical reports on clipboard paper about each of her doll patients. She also set up a school and an office for which she carried on correspondence and listed employees.

A large whiteboard is a good tool for writing while playing "school," practicing the alphabet, studying material for a test, or writing notes. You can leave each other messages on the board.

Or if it's a rainy day and your child is bored, you can write a list of activities that might be fun.

reasons to write

If we give our children good reasons to write, they're more likely to try their hand at it. The following are some activities you can suggest to your child. Pick the ideas best suited to your child's age, personality, and stage of development:

Make place cards for special family dinners and decorate them with stickers, magazine cutouts, or an original picture.

Help your child make an "All About Me" scrapbook. Let him choose ten to fifteen pictures of himself taken from infancy to the present and place them in chronological order. Then he can tape or glue the pictures in a scrapbook or on folder pages. He can write, or dictate for you to write, a caption to go underneath each photo.

Encourage list making: grocery lists, lists of what he will need to complete his science project, birthday wish lists, lists of things he will need for his weekend camping trip, lists of friends to invite to a party, lists of his homework assignments, and lists of daily chores.

Have your child make maps and write directions to a friend's house, to church, to school, or for your next trip. Write directions for things he knows how to do, such as making a birdhouse, planting and growing a flower from a seed, or preparing his favorite dish.

Create a treasure hunt. For Nicholas, one boy I knew, this was his favorite writing activity. He made a whole string of clues on slips of paper for his cousin to follow: "Your next clue is found in the living room by something green." "Now look under the bed." "Beside the dog's bed is your treat." This game was not only "rewarding" it also encouraged him to learn to think through the clues in logical order—and now he has a real gift for sequential reasoning.

Teach your child to make birthday, Valentine's Day, and Christmas cards, writing his own greeting or verse in each one. He can create his own original birthday party invitations, decorate them with colorful stickers, and address the envelopes in his very own handwriting.

Suggest that your child write a script for a puppet show. Using homemade sock puppets and providing various voices for the characters, he can perform it on a rainy day.

Have your child write his own menu and play "restaurant." He can make a sign with the name of the restaurant and then act as a waiter by taking orders on a notepad.

Put together a family newsletter, with each member of the family contributing stories or recent happenings, funny sayings, cartoons, and illustrations. Help your child make photocopies of the letter and send it out. You could also make it an e-newsletter.

story writing and book making

One of the most powerful language activities is to make a book out of a story your child has dictated to you. It could be her own version of "Little Red Riding Hood" or a made-up story. In dictating, she learns that her ideas can be put down on paper with symbols (words). She begins to understand what writing is, and this understanding sparks her interest in expressing herself on paper. Read your child's story back to her just as she dictated it. Soon she'll want to do the writing herself and you can help her make her own books with pictures and homemade bindings.

Diana Purser, a high school English teacher at Zweibrucken High School, located on an American air base in Germany, told me that the best thing she ever did to encourage her daughter's writing was to make a book out of her stories:

> When April was about four years old, we did our first "book" together. It was three pieces of typing paper, trimmed and stapled. April dictated a story to me about a princess in a castle. She drew and colored some pictures to go with the story. It was a small book, but a great beginning! April loved it, and we still have it in her baby book. She created other books, but that first one remained the favorite.

Avoid harshly correcting your child's invented spelling (writing words down as she hears them before she knows the correct spelling). There is a great deal of evidence to indicate that when children invent spelling, they don't necessarily spell words the same way twice. So you don't have to worry that a mistake in spelling made by a five- or six-year-old will be forever ingrained in the child's mind if you allow it to go uncorrected. At the earliest stages, children's writing is much like their drawing—simply a means of self-expression. As they begin to read more, gradually they will begin to incorporate conventional spelling into their writing. Spelling is a developmental skill. By fourth or fifth grade, children have learned how to spell most of the words they need to express their ideas in writing, so they soon learn to edit and revise their own work.

Encourage your child to read her writing aloud and she'll develop a sense of audience. This is the first step in learning to revise.

letter writing and e-mail

Whether it's on postcards, on notebook paper, or in e-mails, letter writing provides one of the best reasons for kids to write. Our son Justin wrote letters to friends in Pennsylvania, Hawaii, and Minnesota, and later, girlfriends he met at summer camp. Alison wrote to friends in New Mexico and Texas. When we moved to Maine, we all wrote to friends and family back home in Oklahoma, and our kids loved to see letters in the mailbox addressed just to them.

Using e-mail is a great way for children to develop writing skills. Kids can e-mail the Library of Congress for material they need for a report on the American Revolution. They can submit a poem or story to a children's magazine, send a thank-you note to Grandma for a birthday gift, or develop a pen-pal friendship with a missionary kid in another country—all via e-mail.

When Andrew, a sixth-grader from Oregon, wanted to keep in touch with his older brother studying in Germany one summer, they e-mailed every other day. Andrew's brother would describe a site he'd visited that day and some history about it, and Andrew would share news of his activities. Over the summer, Andrew's keyboarding and writing skills improved dramatically from the frequent online letter writing. Likewise, a homeschool teen I met at a conference had thirty e-mail pen pals all over the world who supplied her with weekly writing practice.

I've noticed that some kids, particularly teenagers, use the computer in the same way we used to use the telephone and television: for daily gossip sessions and entertainment. As parents, we want to encourage writing on the computer, but we need to realize there's a big difference between composing a letter or research paper and the kind of chatty "instant messaging" that many kids engage in. The latter is certainly communication, but I wouldn't necessarily count it as enriched "writing" time. If your kids spend a lot of time instant messaging or surfing the Internet, it's best to encourage some genuine writing along the way, especially in the form of e-mails they can compose to long-distance family and friends.

Sometimes kids write their e-mails with a shorthand that bypasses most writing practices. They may use all capitals, or no capitals whatsoever. They often avoid punctuation and use lots of acronyms. (For example, "BTW" means "by the way," "LOL" means "laughing out loud," "RME" means "rolling my eyes.") Teachers have even seen this type of writing showing up in class papers—with no indication that the kids realize the difference between Netspeak and proper English. Discuss with your children these netiquette suggestions:

- Use whole words, complete sentences, capital letters, and correct punctuation.

- Respond to your e-mail promptly and politely.

- Use salutations, such as "Dear Aunt Kathy," and an appropriate closing, such as "Sincerely, Lisa" or "Your friend, Jan."

- Don't write in ALL CAPITAL LETTERS. It's just like shouting!

Also, provide guidelines and ground rules for your children's computer and Internet usage. Tom, a Kentucky dad, allowed his son Kyser to e-mail a friend he met at summer camp, but he set some wise computer rules: Ask for permission before you log on; anything dealing with adult language or sites is off-limits; and never give out personal information such as home address or telephone number. He and his son moved from joint sessions in which he showed Kyser how to log on, use the computer, and research on the Internet to Dad reading a book nearby and checking on Kyser while he e-mailed his friend and surfed for computer games. Tom stayed involved with his son's online activities and set a limit on the amount of time Kyser could be on the computer. He also made sure their Internet server provided a filter to block pornography and adult material.

journal writing

A journal is a record of ideas and thoughts kept in a book reserved for that purpose. Let your child pick one out—cloth, spiral, or any type of notebook. Encourage your child to choose a title for the journal: "Jimmy's Jottings," "Sophie's Slices of Life." Explain that the journal can be used as a diary that lists daily events, or it can be used for anything the child wants to write. Some kids like to record favorite sayings, poems, lists of projects to do or places to visit, sketches, hopes and dreams, curious questions, and opinions about movies or books. You could encourage a few minutes of journal writing every day or several times a week, perhaps writing in your own journal at the same time. Journals are not only wonderful for getting into the habit of writing but they also will be treasured keepsakes of childhood later on.

learning logs

A log is a practical learning tool for students of any age. It's a type of writing that might appeal to science- and math-oriented kids who aren't interested in writing poetry or stories. They can keep an ongoing record of what they are learning as it takes place, thus encouraging both thinking and writing skills. After a nature walk, your child can write a log of the autumn things he saw and collected. An older student can record the methods and results of a rocket experiment. Another child may keep a log of the weather over a certain period of time. In a learning log, the child can describe problems, note discoveries, clarify concepts, and record ideas for future projects. This is a great way to get kids to write without their realizing it.

encouraging young writers

Whatever kind of writing our kids are doing, whether at home or school, they need our encouragement rather than a steady diet of criticism. One way to show we value written expression is to keep a file of our children's writing. We can display the writing on the refrigerator or bulletin board for a time and then put it into a file labeled with the particular child's name and the year in which he wrote it. At the end of the year, this writing file can be saved along with other important keepsakes. Then a new file of writing can be started for the next year. Just the simple fact that we're saving their writing shows that it matters to us what they think and create. Kids are usually amazed at how much their writing has progressed from year to year.

When we respond as sensitive, attentive readers to the ideas our children express in writing, their writing efforts are validated. When your child reads his writing aloud, ask good questions such as, "What else can you tell me about this story?" "What's going to happen next?" and "How did you find out about this?" Take a positive approach and always find something good to say about what your child has written. When it's a school assignment, before you give suggestions for revising, notice what they did *right* in the paper—the descriptive words used, the interesting twist at the end of the story, the neat handwriting. Remember that writing is a process, and that if errors are pointed out too soon, too harshly, or too often, children won't keep trying to write. Treating their writing with respect fosters a good self-image and a sense of trust.

Given the proper encouragement, role modeling, and resources, your child can become a fluent writer not just during his school years but throughout his life.

6

music and your
child's learning

There's a resource in your home and a gift you can give your child that doesn't cost a lot of money yet packs a lot of potential to enhance your child's learning. It's the gift of music.

Many studies over the past few decades have shown the power and impact of music on kids' education. Music can make a big difference in your child's growth and development.[1] It advances all the learning systems—in reading, math, logical and creative thinking, and the arts. It enhances language and communication skills, strengthens memory, and paves the way for better fluency in foreign languages. Music lessons help kids develop the discipline and self-confidence they need to succeed in school. Participating in music helps improve a child's attention span, auditory development, and hand-eye coordination.

Whether it is piano, violin, French horn, or drums, the daily practice it takes to play a musical instrument develops patience and perseverance and contributes to kids' pursuing and achieving in higher education. In fact, children and teens who participate in their school orchestra or band are 52 percent more likely to go to college, succeed, and graduate. Students who participated in music either at school or outside of school scored on the average twenty to forty points higher on the Scholastic Aptitude Test (SAT), a college entrance exam.[2]

Even in the early years, music promotes a child's learning. One of the first researchers to discover the positive effects of music on kids' brain development was physicist Gordon Shaw from the University of California, Irvine. In preschools in California, he divided the groups of children into those who received piano and singing lessons and those who participated in art, computer, or other enrichment activities.

What he found after only six months was that the kids who previously had scored in the average range on a standardized test of spatial reasoning scored 34 percent above average after their music experiences. Their overall mental ability, especially in math and logical thinking, was enhanced. The kids who were not given an opportunity to take piano and singing lessons showed no improvement in their test scores.[3] Wouldn't you have wanted your child to be in the fortunate group taking music lessons?

From this and many other studies, experts believe that music participation and training at an early age and throughout childhood are some of the best ways to develop higher cognitive abilities that spur on achievement in math and science. Music is processed in the same part of the brain that logical, mathematical, and scientific thought processes take place, so music participation stimulates growth in that area. Exercising the brain through music strengthens other intellectual skills. It's like exercising your body by jogging, lifting weights, or strength training in order to heighten your ability to play football or soccer.

benefits of classical music

Even the type of music you listen to in your home is important to your child's development and learning. Although there are many wonderful types of music, one of the best forms for your child to listen to is classical. Now, I know many of us aren't in the habit of listening to Bach, Beethoven, Mozart, and Vivaldi, but some studies have shown that the structured, complex melodies of classical music warm up the brain and enhance learning because they're similar to the complex neurological patterns of brain activity that occur when the brain is at peak learning levels. In one study, college kids who listened to a Mozart piece for ten minutes before taking a test scored 30 percent higher than when they had ten minutes of silence, repetitive music, or relaxation tapes.[4]

From the earliest years, you can take advantage of the benefits of classical music. Hearing a Vivaldi piano concerto can be a good way for your baby to relax at naptime. Playing a lively march or the symphonic "Scheherazade" by Nicolai Rimsky-Korsakov, or Brahms' fun, rhythmic "Hungarian Dance No. 5" in the morning helps everyone get a good start on the day before heading for school and work. You can find the music of Beethoven, Bach, and other classical composers at discount stores and children's learning stores, often for a very low price. Tuning in to the classical music station instead of hearing the negative news on talk radio takes no extra time. Kids who have the opportunity to listen to classical music when they're young tend to develop good taste in music and be more discerning in their choice of music when they are the ones buying the CDs.

wiring the brain

Researchers have found that the way these early music experiences wire the brain is somewhat like the way a technician rewires a radio or a computer engineer builds circuitry in a computer. Every time kids have a musical experience, a kind of mapping goes on. In that mapping process, one neuron connects to another and then another and so on—laying down tracks consisting of millions of neurons and creating a "train" of music behaviors. This train will be ready to run for the lifetime of the child. As the number of musical experiences kids have increases, the length of the "track" they have to work with increases. And not only does this mapping affect their ability to play a Beethoven concerto or write an original song, it also carries over to arithmetic skills, analytical thinking, and spatial-visual development.

helping your child grow musically

Music is also valuable for its own sake. There is so much joy in making and listening to good music that even if there were no other benefits, it would still be worth it to sing songs together and play instruments. There are numerous inexpensive, fun ways you can introduce your child to music. Here are a few:

Have fun with music. Turn on music and dance, skip, and hop to different rhythms with your child. Twirl your baby to a happy tune. Hold hands with your preschooler and skip to the music on your CD. It doesn't take much encouragement for her to join in and get in the swing of things.

Music can be a great tool for bonding between parents and kids. As we rock our babies to sleep and sing lullabies, dance with them to *The Nutcracker Suite*, or sing to them while we're changing their diapers and running errands, music enriches our family relationships and builds emotional connections. Playing quiet, peaceful music can help kids relax when they're wound up; lively, upbeat music can lift their spirits when they're feeling sad.

Use rhythm instruments. Making or buying rhythm instruments can be a good investment in your child's musical enjoyment. Children can use simple rhythm instruments such as melody bells, triangles, tambourines, maracas, or drums when they're toddlers and all the way through elementary school. Turn the music on and have your child beat time to the rhythm. Begin with something that has a consistent rhythm, such as a march. Encourage marching to the music while beating time to the music. Then progress to other kinds of music.

If you don't have rhythm instruments, you can make them from things you have in your kitchen. Round oatmeal containers make great drums; rice in a plastic container with a tight lid becomes a shaker; two wooden spoons are clackers. Spread an array of pots, pans, lids, and large spoons on your kitchen floor and see what your toddler does with them.

Give your child the opportunity to play an instrument. One of the best ways to help your child find an instrument she's interested in is to take her to symphony productions or live musical performances. This could involve watching a guitarist at a local restaurant, going to a local Scottish festival with bagpipes and folk instruments, or attending a children's orchestra recital or college string ensemble. When kids see musicians playing, they often get interested in learning a certain instrument. Five-year-old Nicole, the daughter of a friend of mine, heard a flute solo in a local symphony orchestra production. She was captivated and decided she wanted to play the flute. It was a memorable moment in her young life when, after the program, she was able to tell the flutist how much she had enjoyed his music.

If your child takes music lessons, get involved and show your support. One of the most motivating factors in children's music study is parental involvement. Part of the great success of the Suzuki program of music study is that when the child takes classes, the parent is included in lessons and practice sessions. It is a shared learning experience.

Find a daily practice routine and time that work for your and your child's schedule. If she gets in a slump and wants to quit, there are things you can do to help: Talk to the music teacher about changing the music to a piece that would be really fun; appreciate and praise your child's efforts in practice even if she's not advancing as fast as you'd like; and most of all, look for reasons for your child to play and share her music with the family and others outside of lessons—such as playing the piano at a family reunion, entertaining nursing home residents with her instrument, or playing a duet or with a group at school or church. Getting comfortable with performing and seeing the joy their music can bring to others can motivate kids to go the distance with their music study.

Play informally and learn at home. If you play an instrument (or did at one time), dust it off and play it for your child. You may think you play badly, but your child will be delighted with your songs. It will show her that ordinary people—not just famous rock stars or professionals—play instruments. And there's nothing better than everybody getting out their instruments (including rhythm instruments) and having a family music night.

Certain instruments can be learned even without formal lessons. Recorders (a two-octave range flute-like instrument made from wood or molded plastic), guitars, bongo drums, keyboards, harmonicas, and other instruments can be learned with instruction books and curiosity. Your home computer can also be used for learning music from elementary through advanced levels.

Tap in to school music programs and lessons. Many elementary schools offer classes in a variety of instruments. Some include piano lessons. Middle schools and high schools have bands and orchestras your child can participate in. Playing with their peers motivates kids and helps them learn teamwork and cooperation.

When your child is learning an instrument, avoid demanding technical excellence too soon or living through her by demanding musical success. That's a sure way to throw cold water on her interest in music. Let your child's success in music as well as other areas be a reflection of her own desire to achieve. Be patient with toddlers' and preschoolers' music noise so they will become music makers and music lovers for a lifetime.

using music to enhance study

Some kids need and prefer quiet when they're reading, but others find that background music helps them focus. For kids who find music a help rather than a distraction, try playing soft classical music in the background when they are studying or reading to enhance learning and help them concentrate. It works much better than rap or pop music!

You can also use music to improve your child's memory. For example, show her how to remember vowels by setting them to the tune of "Old MacDonald": "Old MacDonald had a farm—A, E, I, O, U." One of my friends learned the whole preamble of the Constitution by singing it. Most of us learned the ABC's by singing them. I learned the books of the Bible by singing them and have memorized Spanish vocabulary words as well as many dates in history by setting them to a tune.

Music is a powerful component of learning. That's why doctors have found that even when people have lost the ability to speak because of a stroke or head injury, they can learn language all over again when phrases and sentences are set to music. Elderly Alzheimer's and dementia patients who haven't spoken a word in years will begin to sing the lyrics when they hear a song they sang in their younger years. Whether it's verbal or numerical information, music can help your child store the material in her long-term memory and recall it when she needs it.

developing math skills

We were a game-playing family. I watched and learned from my big sisters and proudly graduated from Go Fish and Old Maid to Hearts, Monopoly, and Parcheesi. We (the three babies, as the rest of the family called us) had to become really competent players to be allowed to share the deck of cards with the three "big girls." Games such as Simon Says, I Spy, and Mother May I? occupied our spare time, and the game of jacks was not only fun but also kept us in touch with basic math skills. Then there was the magic of jumping rope. Myriad jump-rope counting games kept us hopping up and down, trying to be the winner.

We didn't know that in all these playtime activities, we were learning valuable math concepts such as counting, sequencing, combining, sorting, and problem solving. And none of us ever had much difficulty in math.

> *Arithmetic is where the answer is right and every-thing is nice and you can look out the window and see the blue sky—or the answer is wrong and you have to start all over and try it again and see how it comes out this time.*
>
> —Carl Sandburg, "Arithmetic"

Maybe, like me, you have one child who loves math and another who prefers literature. One finds math easy and fun, and one struggles with all those problems assigned for homework. Whatever your children's bents or aptitudes, there are ways to help them develop good math skills by taking advantage of all the opportunities around you in everyday life.

Claudia Zaslavsky, teacher and author, said, "Some people complain, 'I don't have a mind for math.' We know now that every person has a mind for math, provided the math is presented in an understandable manner. Research has shown that children of all ethnic backgrounds, girls as well as boys, are equally capable of learning mathematics."[1]

But even though most kids can become good students in math, many of them enter the classroom doubting their ability. Math teachers agree that one of the biggest obstacles to children's success in math is not *aptitude* but the *attitude* they bring into the classroom.

Vicki Hamilton, a middle-school math teacher from Dallas, Texas, says, "Try to make sure that you do not create an 'out' for your child by telling him, 'It's okay to do poorly in math; I wasn't good in it either.'" Telling your child you hated math is a surefire way to undermine his learning by instilling in him a negative attitude.

Instead, let your kids see the projects and tackle challenges that utilize math: bookkeeping involved with your job, measuring and timing baked goods, balancing your checkbook, and using coupons at the grocery store. Encourage them to talk with you about your work.

Because kids love to imitate their parents, a little of your positive role modeling can go a long way. One mom I know brought her daughter with her to her part-time bookkeeping job at a clothing store. Her daughter insisted upon having her own ledger and receipt book to fill out. She spent hours writing numbers in her "office books" and acquired an early interest in math.

Help your children become comfortable with math by having them count flavors at the ice cream store and add coins to their piggy bank. Be aware of the math all around you and seize opportunities to share with your children the importance of mathematics. Let them see that it's practical and relates to real life. You can point out that numbers are everywhere and that we use them constantly—often without even thinking about it. Then numbers will make more sense and computing will be more natural in the classroom.

Playing sports is a perfect way for children to see math in everyday life. If your kids are sports-minded, call attention to batting averages, game strategies, and plays in football. Point out the numbers on soccer, basketball, and football uniforms.

Then there's money, money, money! I've rarely met a kid who wasn't interested in dollars and coins, no matter how young they were. I was amazed at how early Caitlin and Caleb, two of our grandchildren, knew the difference between quarters, nickels, and dimes. In addition, we can point out that math used when measuring is important whether we are cooking, climbing a mountain, riding a bike, building a doghouse, or sewing.

We can also talk about all the occupations that use math and for which math is a prerequisite: computer fields; architecture; science; business management; engineering; aerospace; and medical, surgical, and nursing fields. I'm not suggesting you drop a "Math Is Important" lecture on your kids in one fell swoop and expect them to suddenly become math-oriented. Instead, you can share informally with your children as you demonstrate the value of math skills in everyday life.

make math fun

Kids are natural mathematicians. Believe it or not, even five-month-old babies have a basic ability to perceive quantities and a rudimentary ability to add and subtract. Researchers have found that older babies can distinguish at just a glance the difference between one, two, three, and four balls.[2] By kindergarten, kids have many math ideas under their thinking caps—they understand largest and smallest, longer and shorter, closest and farthest. They can count objects as they touch them, and some can even count to ten or higher. Kids are much smarter than we think—especially in math.

Young children learn best from hands-on activities in which they're using math for real reasons. Even before they can ever do a math workbook, they hop on every other brick or touch every other fence post and sing rhymes such as "One, Two, Buckle My Shoe." Kids learn to count naturally if they have concrete things to count. Even in elementary math, they need objects to count and manipulate until they have reached a certain level of abstract ask, "How much gas will we need to fill the tank?" or "What is the speed limit?" Older children can help figure out how long it would take to drive instead of fly to Grandma's.

Counting toys: Count toys while putting them away on shelves or in bins.

Puzzles and blocks: Puzzles give practice in identifying shapes and matching colors. Blocks teach many math concepts: weight, size, spatial relationships, order, and proportion.

Reading a calendar: "How many days until your birthday? Let's count them." An Advent calendar is a fun way to learn bout the Advent season and count off the days until the arrival Christmas.

Comparing sizes and amounts: "Which apple is bigger?" "How oranges does it take to make a pound?"

asuring height: "Who is tallest: Dad, Mom, or Sister?" Use tape to record your child's height.

ng number songs: "Five Frogs Sitting on a Log," "Ten ns," "Five Little Pumpkins," "Three Little Monkeys."

: Libraries are full of delightful picture books that math concepts. Some suggested books are: *Arthur's* , by Lillian Hoban; *Caps for Sale*, by Esphyr *e Tenth Good Thing About Barney*, by Judith *ling a House*, by Byron Barton.

Play "restaurant" or "store" using real coins.

vocabulary: Using numbers naturally when ts helps build your children's math vocabu- grapes for you! Eat one. Now three take thinking. Children who are pushed too early into abstract mathematical concepts (numbers on paper) often develop "math phobia." Such children display little motivation for math, dislike it for no apparent reason, and seem to show their lack of affinity for the subject by doing poorly on math tests.

But you can make math fun, more like a puzzle than a chore. As early as infancy, you can begin to introduce your children to math by counting aloud their fingers and toes, singing nurse rhymes and songs that involve counting, and counting the tons on their sweater while dressing them.

Here are more ways to build a solid foundatior children (these suggestions apply to children f through age eight):

Sorting: Let your children sort laundry, They can sort silverware, putting knives their proper slots. (Categorizing is a b

Setting the table: "Let's count k tonight for dinner." "Where does is foundational to math skills

Cooking: Most children process, they learn ab dividing portions.

Telling time: "r special?" "How one good-siz

*Getting from store or to the hous

away one leaves how many? One, two!" "Do you want your cheese sandwich cut into halves or fourths?" Then demonstrate. As you interact with your kids—counting toys and objects, sorting and playing with shapes—they'll be developing positive attitudes toward math.

Games and cards: There are plenty of games for building math skills. A deck of playing cards offers children opportunities to match suits and numbers, count, and practice logic and problem solving. Young children can also play simple games of Concentration, Go Fish, Old Maid, Slapjack, or War.

It may seem like they're just having fun, but don't underestimate the power of playing card games with kids. Child psychologist Dr. Margie Golick told of a six-year-old who, after a year in kindergarten and half a year in first grade, was still unable to remember which number was which. He was easily distracted, clumsy, and spatially confused. Dr. Golick taught the child to play Go Fish. After a week of playing the game, the six-year-old was able to master instant recognition of numbers one to ten.[3]

Dr. Golick pointed out that an inexpensive deck of cards is the best educational tool available for teaching a child the essential math concepts of sorting and grouping; space, time, and number; and logic and problem solving. For the learning-disabled child, card games are particularly helpful because they motivate him "to work at something over and over again just because it is so intriguing, so challenging, or so much fun."[4]

Crazy Eights, Spades, and Hearts are great card games to play with children of elementary age or older. Just one game of

Hearts, for instance, provides practice in many learning skills that are essential to success in math: categorizing, counting, judging rank of numbers, considering several factors at once, adding, reasoning, using memory, calculating probabilities, and developing strategies.

Your children's math skills can also be developed by playing games such as beanbag toss, dominoes, bowling, Monopoly, Clue, chess, and Battleship.

computer games

Computer games can provide a great reason for kids to practice and build their math skills. For example, Math Munchers Deluxe is a computer game that reinforces basic math skills. Kids help the Math Munchers dodge a crew of troublesome Troggles and, in the process, develop skills in addition, subtraction, multiplication, division, whole numbers, and more. The game also challenges kids' minds in the areas of comparing, classifying, and encoding.

Math Blaster provides practice in basic arithmetic facts, fractions, decimals, and percentages. Zoombini's Logical Journey is an entertaining computer program that builds and strengthens important reasoning and mathematical communication skills. Kids also hone graph-reading skills, learn prealgebra basics, and learn how to sort, organize, and analyze data—all while they're having fun.

The Lemonade Stand is a computer game that gives children opportunities to learn business skills as they order their materials, practice using money, and develop a little entrepreneurial mind-set at the same time.

To find new math games for free, use any Internet search engine, type in "math games," and then click on a link to a website that provides learning opportunities through computer math.

memorizing math facts

One of the most important math skills for elementary school children is the ability to memorize addition, subtraction, multiplication, and division facts. Without this skill, kids are handicapped in junior high school math and beyond. There are many daily tasks—computing costs at the grocery store, gas mileage, and insurance premiums—in which one needs to know what, for example, 7 x 5 equals. These math facts are taught at school, but most students need a little help from parents and practice at home if they are to gain complete mastery on schedule.

Memorizing is always easier with two people—child and child, parent and child, or tutor and child. Drills, practice, and usage make these facts easier to retain and recall when needed.

You can make memorizing math facts more fun by using homemade or store-bought flash cards. Because most kids today like working on the computer, you might want to find online flash cards by typing "math flash cards" into any Internet search engine.

Addition/Subtraction Bingo, Multiplication Bingo, and other math games you can buy at learning stores promote math fact retention. You can also quiz your children when you're driving to school or running errands—working on twos, threes, fives, or whichever set of multiplication facts is weakest.

Encourage your kids to make up their own math games. Our daughter, Alison, invented a multiplication Mother May I? game in the third grade. I would hold up a flash card with a math fact (such as 9 x 7) on it. If she got the answer right, she took one step forward; if her answer was wrong, she had to take one step backward. We went through a whole stack of multiplication facts. She learned them well enough to make an A on the speed drills at school.

what about calculators?

During the elementary school years, children are still learning basic computational facts and need to develop their personal math skills before allowing a calculator to do the work for them. During regular classroom hours and in their home study, it is best for them to do their own "calculating." Calculators have a place in math and can be very handy but should be introduced after children have mastered the basics. Knowledge of the proper use of a calculator is essential in our electronic society, but it needs to come at the right stage of development.

Lynn Fuller, who has instructed kids for twenty-five years, advises that through fourth-grade math, students shouldn't rely on a calculator to do their thinking. Learning multiplication skills teaches them many concepts, such as understanding what a perfect square is. Knowing multiplication tables will save them time in figuring square roots and percentages. In trigonometry and higher-level math, the calculator is a valuable tool that saves time and helps students focus on higher-thinking skills.

The exceptions for calculator use in elementary grades might be occasional problem-solving and challenge activities, in which the emphasis is placed on "how-to" skills, not on basic computation. Let your children use a calculator for fun and motivation. Allow them to use it to check their work. But if they find that an answer is wrong, they should rework the problem themselves before using the calculator to recheck it.

math enrichment for the middle school years

By middle school, your child can add, subtract, multiply, and divide. Here are some ways to provide opportunities for him to use and practice these skills and more:

Experiment with estimating. When students can make good estimates of the answer to an arithmetic problem, it shows they understand the problem. This skill leads them to reject unreasonable answers and to know whether they are in the ballpark.[5] One way to work on estimating is with shopping skills. Let your child estimate the cost of the items on your grocery list by adding up the prices listed in the newspaper food ads and then deducting for any coupons. If you see a half-price sale, have your child help you figure the prices. At the grocery store, if bananas are three pounds for a dollar, ask her to figure how much it will cost to buy one pound, two pounds, or five pounds.

Be an entrepreneur. Let your child have a lemonade or cookie stand, hold a toy sale, or assist in a garage sale. He can help you price objects to be sold and act as your cashier.

Play mental math. This is a great brain-boosting activity. When you're driving in the car, ask your child a continuous problem (age-appropriate) to be figured out in his head rather than on paper. For example: 2 plus 5 times 6 minus 7 times 3 minus 4 equals what? This exercise challenges my brain too! Choose only addition and subtraction for a first- or second-grader and more advanced math operations for an older child.

Set up a budget. Setting up a budget can make math skills practical and meaningful. Start with a goal, such as the purchase of a certain much-wanted toy. Have your child find out how much money it will take to reach that goal and how much of his weekly allowance he can save. Then brainstorm with him on ways for him to earn that amount by doing special jobs.

Practice using percentages. One of the most difficult concepts in middle school math is percentage. Give your child practical, concrete percentage problems to figure out. One teacher's most successful project is allowing her seventh-graders to design a sale circular. She gives them the items to be included, their original price, and the percentage of the markdown. Then they have to figure the sale price and incorporate all the necessary information into a circular ad.

Combine math and maps. Use travel as a way of practicing math skills. Your child can use a map to determine how far it is to your vacation destination and then figure the amount of total transportation costs, taking into account the differences in camping fees, motel rates, and gasoline prices.

Work math puzzles. Math puzzles come in paperback books and are enjoyable and challenging ways to practice math skills.

i'm stuck!

Let's face it: Every now and then, our kids are going to face a difficult set of math problems. What if they get stuck? What if you have difficulty explaining the problem? The paragraphs that follow are full of good homework strategies to help your child with math.

If the math assignment is long or unusually difficult, set a kitchen timer for twenty or thirty minutes and have your child work for that set period of time. At the sound of the alarm, let him take a break and come back later to finish the assignment. Or if he comes home totally overwhelmed by the large number of problems he has been assigned, spread them out. Have him work one-fourth of them after school, one-fourth right before dinner, one-fourth after dinner, and one-fourth before bedtime.

When the assignment covers a new lesson or a concept he's struggled with, you might have your child do three or four of the assigned problems. Then check those and have him do eight or ten more. This prevents him from doing a whole lesson wrong.

If your child is really stuck, he might need a little push. Don't let an obstacle become an excuse to quit. Show him how to do a similar problem and then see if he can handle the original troublesome one. Instead of giving your child the answer, ask questions to walk him through each step of the problem. For example, "What do you think we should try first? Okay, let's make up a simpler problem and see if that will work. Good, that should work here too. Now what will we do next?" Or "That didn't work quite right. What other way can we try?"

If you feel one way of explaining a concept isn't working, try another way, such as using manipulatives—rocks, blocks, counting bears, or something concrete your child can use to understand the abstract math concept. Drawing pictures or graphs can help the idea click. For some kids, it helps to have them start at the beginning and explain to you what the teacher taught in class concerning this type of problem. Listen for confusion or misinformation, and work the child toward understanding. Explain orally, and then turn the tables and let him teach you how to do a problem.

If you've done all the explaining you can and your child's still not making progress, consider sending the child in for extra help from his teacher or tutor once a week.

reaping the benefits

Inequalities, proportions, algebraic solutions, and other advanced math concepts—your child can tackle all of these better if he has a strong foundation in number concepts gained by working and playing with concrete objects when he's young; he has a positive attitude about the value of math; he masters the math facts and basic concepts, such as estimating, rounding, place value, and decimals; and he has developed good study habits and test-taking skills. It sounds like an impossible dream, but it's really a step-by-step process.

8

encouraging good
study habits

One year, Steven sat in the back of my freshman English class. He had one of the highest IQs in the class and loved science fiction. However, instead of doing his homework, he stayed up late, sometimes until 2:00 AM, playing with his computer. He had no set study hours and no schedule for sleeping. He was on his own to do whatever he felt like. Rather than following a planned, balanced diet, he preferred stuffing himself at all hours with sugar-laden junk food. As a result of his poor eating, sleeping, and study habits, Steven was often drowsy and listless in class. Consequently, in spite of his high IQ, he was failing not only English but also most of his other ninth-grade courses—and becoming depressed in the process.

Steven is a prime example of the fact that just having a high IQ doesn't ensure success in school. The way children study and the structure provided at home has a major impact on how much they learn. Researchers have found that the parents of successful students take time to help their children develop effective study strategies.

lowering the boom

For many years while teaching junior high school and high school English, I saw parents "lower the boom" on their kids the last four or five days of the nine-week grading period, when it was almost too late to recover. "You're grounded for the next month if you don't make a C in English!" "No TV ever until you bring your grades up in math!" they would say in frustration instead of supporting their children's learning and insisting on good study habits from the first day.

When we're busy and pressured with our own concerns, it's easy to become lax about our kids' study habits. We assume they're doing just fine and hope for the best. Sometimes we get out of touch with their teachers, miss a conference, or don't have time to check that they are turning in their assignments on time. We skate along until a warning slip from their teacher arrives in the mail or they bring home a report card full of low grades.

what is the parent's role in homework and study?

I have a friend who by second grade had been placed in a remedial reading group. His mom began to tutor him at home and insisted he couldn't go outside and play until his homework was all done. As a result of her efforts, he learned good study habits. He also had chores to do on Saturday and became actively involved in sports and church activities, contributing to his sense of responsibility.

This young man reached the top of his class and stayed there right through college, where he was an honors premed student and excelled in medical school. Today, he is a successful surgeon. He credits his academic success to his mom's hard-nosed attitude and unbending rule "Work first—play later."

Here are ways you can support your children in developing good study habits and enjoying academic success:

Promote a positive attitude toward schoolwork. Let your kids know that hard work pays off and that schoolwork is a priority. Homework overload is a hot topic because homework loads have increased, and some parents feel it's too much. The more-homework camp thinks that the increases in homework time raises standardized test scores and gets kids into better colleges. But with too much homework, many kids get burned out and parents get stressed out.

I think a moderate amount of homework is good for kids and parents. It builds study habits and reinforces the day's assignments. And the best benefit may be that it not only helps you stay up with what your kids are learning in the classroom but also shows that you value your children's learning. Homework is one of your best connecting points with the teacher, the school, and your children. A review of research studies shows that it's parental interest in homework that makes test scores go up rather than just the fact that kids are doing the homework.

Whether your children find the homework load positive or burdensome, the bottom line is that it's your responsibility to help your kids cope with the workload and get through it. Complaining in front of them that the teacher has assigned too much work tends to be counterproductive because your attitude has a huge impact on your kids' attitudes. The place to appeal is privately in a conference with the teacher, principal, administration, or Parent-Teacher Association (PTA). In the meantime, help your children manage their time so they can get the homework done.

Praise your children's efforts. Every child should experience some success, however small, every day. Pay attention to what your children do right, and give genuine praise when it is due instead of focusing on what they're not doing well. "I appreciate your hard work; I'm proud of you" can mean a lot to children. Avoid bribing them to make better grades or threatening them when they make bad grades. Rewards are great as a surprise and for effort or progress. You can take your son or daughter out for pizza after an improved test score just as you would after a soccer game. Encouraging and acknowledging kids' efforts causes them to try harder, while constant criticism derails their efforts.

Be interested in content, in what your children are learning, not just in their grades. Read a chapter of their textbook or find out a little of what they're learning so you can ask specific questions (always better than the generic question "How was school today?" to which kids usually respond, "Fine.")

Make tasks doable and set realistic goals. Encourage your children to set goals they can reach, such as bringing their history grade up from a C to a B (instead of from an F to an A). Help them break large tasks into smaller steps. For example, if they have a long report to write, have them do the library work this week and write the paper next week.

Encourage self-reliance and responsibility. Your children need your support, but they also need to do their homework themselves. Kids are smart enough to know that if they procrastinate long enough, then their parents will pick up the ball and do their poster for them so they won't get a zero. Remember, it's the students' work, not yours. Better a zero in the fourth grade than your having years of projects and reports to complete and your children growing more and more irresponsible!

It may take a little extra time, but if they have done a math problem incorrectly, avoid redoing it yourself. Show them how to work a similar problem if they truly can't figure it out for themselves. Then let them correct the problem. If they have four glaring run-on sentences in an essay, you could call them to your children's attention and give them an example of how to revise the paper, but let them make the revision. That way you're empowering your child and encouraging self-reliance—an "I can do it" attitude.

Give your children responsibility at home. Teachers say that they can spot a student who has responsibility or chores at home because he does better in class. Encourage your children to take responsibility for their belongings. Have them carry out a few daily chores at home. Require that they keep their room clean enough that you can walk through it without tripping over their possessions. If you can instill a sense of personal responsibility in your kids when they're young, you'll have gone a long way toward helping them become successful in school—and in life.

parent: homework consultant

I like to compare our role as parents to that of a homework *consultant*. Think of yourself as the supervisor, cheerleader, or coach—but not the one who takes ownership for the homework. A consultant advises, helps plan a strategy, provides structure, and makes suggestions for organizational changes.

A friend of ours in Texas hired a consultant to evaluate the method of operation of his clothing store and make recommendations for improvements in every aspect of his business. By following the consultant's advice, our friend saved a great deal of money, made some important changes in his basic operation, and got the business on a firm footing before the outbreak of an expected recession. As a result, he was able to survive—and even increase his share of the market—during a time when many less stable clothing businesses in the area were going bankrupt.

In a similar way, you can provide your children the tools they'll need for school, teach them study strategies that will work for them, and help them get organized.

help kids get organized for school

Don't we wish that all kids were born organized? Don't we wish that we were able to organize all the various facets of our lives, homes, and offices? In truth, organizing is a big challenge, but it's a key to succeeding in school. Disorganization is a leading cause of discouragement and failure in school.

Rachel entered a big public high school after attending a small Christian school for her elementary and junior high years. She was quickly overwhelmed and began turning in her work late and being generally disorganized. Her grades plummeted. Concerned about her low grades, her mom hired a college student to be Rachel's study buddy. For about six bucks an hour, the college student shared her own secrets to high school success and helped Rachel organize her notebook, keep track of assignments, and study for tests. It was worth every penny. As Rachel became more organized, she started enjoying her classes more and her grades improved.

Kids like Rachel who forget where they put their books or assignments have trouble concentrating on their schoolwork. Wouldn't you? It raises their level of anxiety in the classroom and makes it hard to feel prepared. Organized kids feel more confident and do better in every subject.

Some people are natural organizers, like my husband, who color-categorizes his socks in the drawer and keeps all his hangers equidistant in the closet. But most people, especially in the early years, need some help keeping assignments, books, and papers straight. And if your child has a learning problem, it's even more important to teach him organization.

To help your child keep up with assignments, use the following:

A calendar to map out the year with your child. Make a family calendar and mark activities such as band concerts, PTA meetings, and dance recitals. Note due dates of science projects and term papers as well as dates of tests, report cards, field trips, holidays, birthdays, sports games, and church activities.

A pocket calendar, daily planner, or assignment notebook works for some kids. But for someone who needs extra help, make him a weekly calendar sheet of his classes, with boxes for each subject and day of the week. Each week, provide a photocopy of this blank calendar to staple to the front of his main notebook, and have him fill in the appropriate blanks with reminders of upcoming assignments and tests.

Yellow sticky notes to help your child remember to bring home the right books. I'm sure you've heard something like this before: "I forgot my French and science books, and I have homework to do in both of them!" The school is locked, of course. The solution to this problem is to have the student stick a yellow note inside each book he is going to need for homework that evening. At the end of the day, when he sees the yellow tab sticking out of the book, he will be reminded to bring it home.

Accountability sheets. If your child is failing to do his homework because he neglects to write down his assignments (and if he fails to respond to these other methods), there is one final alternative: an accountability sheet. On one sheet per day, the student writes down the assignment and takes it up for the teacher to initial at the end of each class. The homework sheet goes home at the end of the day. The parent checks it to see what assignments need to be done for that day, and a small reward or treat is given when the child completes the assignments successfully. I've seen this method work when other methods have failed. It helps the student become more responsible. By getting assignments done, he brings his grades up, feels better about himself and his ability, and builds a cycle of success instead of failure. Once he gets into the habit of keeping track of his assignments, he can transition to using a regular assignment notebook. Periodically check in with him about his assignments, but by this point, you no longer need to do it on a daily basis.

tools for school

A school-supply shelf is a time-saver at home. Either a cabinet shelf or a plastic bin next to a desk or study area can contain extra ballpoint pens, pencils, erasers, paper, file folders, and markers. Index cards, a stapler and staples, glue, and paper clips are handy items to have available. Also, keep on hand two or three poster boards for special projects. This may save you a trip to the store at 10:00 PM. Having the tools for study is much better than having children borrowing supplies from other students or not having what they need.

a place and time for study

Designate an area for your child to keep books and school stuff. Every person in the family needs a study or work space in the home. An organized desk in a relatively quiet place (without TV, CD player, or video games to distract) with good lighting, containers for supplies, and space to read and write promotes learning. Give your child a yellow or red folder to hold assignments she needs to turn in. Some kids study best at the kitchen table with a parent nearby paying bills, reading, or writing a letter.

Wherever the study place is, encourage your child to go there daily and do homework, read a book, work on a project, or review something that she's going to be tested on later in the week. It takes about four to six days to form a positive pattern for school-age kids. Just as brushing their teeth becomes a habit in the morning and before bedtime, study can become a habit. Then there won't be as much debate over whether to do it or not.

Most children need a break after school and before starting their homework. Their eyes need a rest from so much close work. Intellectually and emotionally, they may be saturated with instructions, activities, and the presence of people, so they may need a little unstructured time and space to unwind, play outside, ride a bike, or throw a ball.

After a break, set the kitchen timer for twenty or thirty minutes (depending on your child's age and attention span) and encourage her to begin her homework. She can take the hardest subject and tackle it first: "Let's see if you can get these ten problems done before the timer goes off." Then after that work is done, she can take perhaps a five-minute break for water or a stretch and then move on to the next subject for twenty or thirty minutes. For most elementary school kids, this may be enough time to finish all of their work. If necessary, the last study period can be delayed until after dinner.

After dinner is a great time to read aloud or play a game. Children should have time to "parachute down" and relax before jumping in bed. A time of togetherness and communication with Mom or Dad prior to going to sleep is extremely supportive to a growing child. Of course, the child needs adequate sleep for her age and individual needs.

Routines like these provide the structure kids need to stay on track during the school year. They're simple things that make a big difference. "A home without any structure," said one learning specialist, "is a home with a high prospect of homework problems."[1] Have a morning routine for waking up and preparing for the day, and make sure each child has her own alarm clock.

Time spent helping your child develop strong study skills while she is in grades one through six will save you much time and frustration later on. The child who learns responsibility, organization, and good study habits will by her junior high school years be quite independent, confident, and able to handle the challenges ahead.

get a great start

To ease your kids into the school year, start getting them up at the right time about a week before it starts. If they ride the bus, show them where the bus stop is. If they'll be attending a different school, arrange a visit to it so it won't be an unfamiliar place on the first day. A week to two weeks ahead of the start of school, teachers are often in their classrooms getting ready. You can call ahead to find out the best time to take your kids to meet the teacher, walk around the hallways, and visit the playground. They'll feel more at home and more confident on the first big day.

Don't forget how important nutrition is for brain development and kids' potential. Children's eating habits can greatly affect their learning potential. They need proteins for alertness, thinking, focusing, increasing metabolism, and building muscle. They need complex carbohydrates such as oatmeal, whole wheat bread, vegetables, and fruit to keep energy up and stimulate serotonin, a brain chemical linked to calmness. Iron is necessary for good concentration. The omega-3 fatty acids or "good fats" found in fish, walnuts, and green leafy vegetables improve kids' brain function and enhance their ability to focus and concentrate on tasks in the classroom. Sending your kids off with a nutritious breakfast and packing a healthful lunch will prepare them to learn and grow during their school days.

9

helping your child
retain information

I have heard lots of creative excuses for homework not being done or students being unprepared for tests: "My dog ate my notes, so I couldn't study for the test," "The computer ate my homework," "My mom spilled chili on my report." I've seen students hide in bathroom stalls or ditch class because they were so anxious about taking a test. Often the real problem is that the kids don't know how to prepare. To do well in school, they need to not only hear information in class or read it in a book but also be able to recall the facts, figures, and other information essential to knowing history, math, English, and other subjects. In other words, they need to be able to retrieve the information out of their mental hard drives! Most students need someone to show them study strategies and how to develop their recall ability in order to do this. Anxiety flees when they can retrieve the words they need to fill in the blank or the numbers to work the math problems. Kids can get more done in less time when they learn techniques that work for them.

Teaching your child a few key study strategies can help him master the building blocks of information and concepts that are presented to him at school and that he'll be tested on. This is especially important because as kids proceed through the grades, the demand on their memories increases. This demand builds up until middle school, where there's a "heavy surge of memory demand—all those scientific facts, historical dates, math processes, and geographic places" they have to file away.[1] Just like a coach standing on the sidelines, laying strategies, offering encouragement, and providing direction when needed, you can "coach" your child to getting the information in and out of his brain and finding success in study—even if he hits some bumps in the road.

going for the gold

Joel threw his book on the table and said, "I just can't do this."

His mom knew he was frustrated with school. The family had moved to Oklahoma City, and their three boys were enrolled in the local public school. The two older boys were adapting well, but their sixth-grader, Joel, was their greatest concern. His elementary school years had been hard, and he'd struggled through fourth and fifth grades. Entering sixth grade at a new school, he'd taken standardized tests and scored only 15 out of 100 in math and 27 out of 100 in language.

Here he was about to give up after only one week in school. His words catapulted his mom, Peggy, into action. She began volunteering in Joel's classroom, and by being there one afternoon a week, she got to know his teachers, saw what they expected of the students, and got supplemental materials for him. Each day after school, they worked together. If the assignment was math, they did half the problems together and Joel did the rest himself. They made flash cards to practice his spelling words each week, and often he read aloud his science and history textbooks, using a globe, atlas, and extra books to enrich the material.

When the science fair came around in the fall, Joel decided on a project, and the family helped him gather materials and cheered him on as he worked. When he took first place in his division, Joel (who'd always felt overshadowed by his high-achieving older brothers) felt his confidence rise. After that, he decided to double his study efforts, "go for the gold," and try to earn straight As. By the fourth quarter of seventh grade, he did it. For the first time ever, Joel made all As. But the biggest improvement was in his standardized test scores: They rose to 98 in math and 89 in language.

Joel's attitude changed from "I can't do this" to "I know I can do it." He persevered through high school and college, often having to work much harder than other classmates to get high grades. At the university, he was a straight-A student, on the president's honor roll, and inducted into an honorary academic fraternity. While pursuing a master's degree, he won a fellowship to study in Europe, got his pilot's license, and now teaches English as a second language at a Japanese university. The boy who struggled with sixth-grade homework has become a lifelong learner for whom the sky's the limit!

There are some ways you too can help your child learn

to study and achieve. It's the "teach a man to fish" principle. You aren't doing the work for him; you're showing him how to learn—and it will pay off in innumerable ways.

taking notes

Taking good notes helps kids retain what they're supposed to remember from class lectures and presentations. It also helps them stay alert, interested, and tuned-in while the teacher is talking, because they're actively doing something with the information they're hearing rather than passively sitting through a lecture or killing time until lunch. When required to sit and listen for a long period of time, very active kids and those who are visually oriented become bored and restless. They tune out mentally and begin to daydream, doodle, or cause problems in class.

Here are some simple suggestions to share with your child about taking notes:

Listen for teacher cues. If the teacher writes facts or concepts on the board, they are probably important and should be written down. She might give verbal clues, such as: "*Three primary causes of the Civil War are . . .*" or "*The purpose of the* Bill of Rights is . . .*" If your child is confused about the most important points, he should ask the teacher about them. If he gets distracted when he's sitting at the back of the room, he should ask to sit closer to the front.

Take notes either in a basic outline form or on index cards. (If you have a method for taking notes that works for you, share it with your child.)

Review the notes at a later time, using a yellow highlighter to mark important points in the notes. When it comes time for a test on the material, your child can study those notes by reading over them several days in advance and then discussing or tape-recording them.

reading and summarizing a chapter

Suggest that your child note key headings and topic sentences as she reads each chapter or section. To help her clarify and retain what she has read, she should ask herself questions about the material such as, *What's the main idea in this paragraph? What am I supposed to be learning? What do I need to remember?*

Then she can highlight the answers to these questions in the textbook, write them in her own words in her notebook, or make a diagram or drawing of the main idea. If she's studying history facts, she might want to create a time line.

A lot of kids can learn by paying attention to headings, introductions, new vocabulary words, and summaries at the ends of chapters. Charts, review questions, and glossaries are good tools for understanding the material. Just *doing* something with the material instead of scanning the words makes a big difference.

memorizing magic

You can take the drudgery out of memorization by making a game of it. Some information—such as multiplication tables, correct spelling of words, dates in history, vocabulary in foreign languages, and parts of speech—needs to be memorized. There are different ways to get the information into the "hard drive" of kids' memories so they can retrieve it at a later time—for instance, on a test. Some memorization strategies link the known to the unknown. Others make use of mental pictures and humor. For many kids, setting the information to music helps them remember it.

Using mnemonics, or memory devices, is another way to make memorizing faster and more fun. For example, in music, teachers encourage students to use "Every Good Boy Does Fine" to recall the order of the treble clef notes on the staff: EGBDF. To remember the names of the Great Lakes, just think of the word HOMES: Huron, Ontario, Michigan, Erie, and Superior. Even med students use mnemonics to memorize everything from bones to assessment techniques.

Whether it involves learning key formulas, state capitals, or other basic facts, you and your child can make up your own devices to increase retention and jog the memory. When kids come up with their own study methods, they tend to remember things better.

studying for tests

The first key is to help your child plan ahead instead of cramming the night before. A few nights before the test, have him review his notes. The second night, he might do something different with the material, such as tape-record the main points or practice the basic information by using flash cards. The night before the test, help him make out a practice test using the type of questions the teacher usually asks. (Most teachers have a pattern to the multiple-choice, true-false, fill-in-the-blank, or essay questions they ask, and it helps to structure the practice test like that.) When kids take a practice test that they helped create, it tends to increase their test-taking confidence as well as their scores. In addition:

Encourage study partners or a study group. Kids can learn a lot from each other. After orally drilling each other on the material, each person in the study group can write down the top three questions he thinks will most likely be on the exam, look up the answers, and discuss them. The group can then pool their information, make up and take a practice test, and score it for each other.

Turn the tables and have your child teach the material he's going to be tested on to younger siblings, to a friend, or to you. Provide a big whiteboard and let him play the teacher's role. I've seen kids' test results go up several letter grades when they get actively involved in teaching the material before a test.

After the test is over, if the score is still low, avoid saying, "I told you so," or criticizing. Sometimes the amount of time and effort put into study is not reflected in the final grade, especially in the first stages of trying out various study strategies. It takes persistence and determination—character traits your child needs to develop not only for school but also for life.

Most of all, praise your child's efforts. Encourage him to press on and keep up with daily work. Help him prepare for the next test.

help: where do i get it?

The best and brightest students have something in common: They know where to turn for assistance when they need it, and they don't hesitate to ask. Most kids are going to need help at some time or another, and learning how to ask for it takes some practice.

Even in elementary school, children need to know that the teacher is there to help them but that it's their responsibility to ask for that help. They may want to go before or after school to talk to the teacher or ask a question. Usually the teacher is glad to help and often feels more positive toward the student because she's showing interest.

Let your child know she also can get help from an older brother or sister who has taken the course, parents, a friend who's a retired teacher or specialist in a pertinent subject, a tutor, or a community learning center that provides evaluation and tutoring services.

the parent-teacher connection

As I raced to my son's next class, the heel of my shoe turned and I slipped on the slick hall floor. A man walking by caught me just before I hit the floor.

"Are you all right?" he asked.

"I don't think I broke anything," I answered. "I'll be okay."

We had only five minutes between bells to find the classes, and this was a big high school building. My foot hurt, and I knew I was going to be late. Suddenly, I knew just how our kids often feel in the stressful world of junior high and high school.

I hurriedly slid into the seat closest to the door in my son's history class just in time to hear the teacher say, "I like to teach ninth-graders, but I'm sure glad they have to go home to you!" Teenagers, she explained, are a handful. Oh, how I knew that—or at least was beginning to find out.

Open House, usually held early in the school year, is one way to meet your child's teachers and start becoming involved with his school. When parents and teachers team up, kids learn best. When you visit your child at school, your involvement shows that his education is important to you. Parents and teachers are supposed to be partners in education, and if we are going to work for the best interests of our children, we need to know our partners.

At Open House, parents may see a sampling of their children's work. At all levels, each teacher gives a presentation about the curriculum and what the students will learn in the class. Often the teacher will explain the grading scale, homework requirements, and goals for the school year. Parents get a sense of the teacher's expectations. But most teachers don't have time to discuss individual students at Open House; instead, it is a get-acquainted time.

I've heard teachers say to parents, "Don't believe everything you hear about me, and I won't believe everything I hear about you!" Effective communication between home and school is vital to avoid misunderstandings—or to clear them up when they do occur. Despite all of our best efforts to make our educational system effective, the truth is that schools are imperfect institutions run by imperfect people who must work with imperfect students. The parents who love those students are imperfect too! Mistakes will be made by all parties involved. But if we build a working relationship with teachers, together we can identify problems and work to solve them before they become detrimental to our children's progress.

It's kind of like getting the fire engine ready before the fire. You don't want to wait until a fire is raging to prepare and equip a fire truck. It's the same way with teachers. There are going to be places you disagree or problems that your child has in a certain teacher's class. If you build a relationship with the teacher before the "fire," when there's a problem, the teacher will know you aren't attacking as a foe but are working together, friend to friend, as a team. We can respect teachers but still deal with the problem and be an advocate for our child.

You may be thinking, *But my child is doing above-average work.* Even if your child is doing well in school, it's helpful to keep the lines of communication open for future needs that may arise. You want to know that your child is being challenged and not just going through the motions. By keeping the lines of communication open with your child's teacher, you can gain important insights into your child's development and how he interacts with peers. You will discover skills that need to be reinforced at home as well as enrichment you can provide outside of the school environment. The teacher needs your interest and support because you're an important part of the team.

building relationships

One of the keys to building relationships with those who teach or coach your kids is to express gratitude for something positive they do. You don't have to be on school premises or take a lot of time to do this relationship-building activity. It just takes a simple note. Think about something that helped or motivated your child, and then thank the teacher for it, such as, "Thanks for the extra help you gave Holly on her math problems and the multiplication table practice sheets you sent home. We think she's gaining more confidence, and we appreciate all you're doing to encourage her."

Many teachers are stressed, feel unappreciated, and go the whole year without a single note that lets them know what they're doing right. Your note of thanks takes only a few minutes but can have a big impact. In these days of e-mail, it is so easy to make a teacher's day.

A friend of mine got amazing results from this suggestion. Melanie sent notes to her daughters' teachers, thanking them for specific things. She thanked Heather's teacher for the individual attention she had given Heather and the positive changes it made to Heather's self-esteem. Melanie thanked Lauren's teacher for making learning to read fun and described the light that beamed in Lauren's eyes when she began recognizing words she was reading.

The teachers received their notes on the day of Open House. That night, Heather's teacher spoke of how she wanted to work on elevating her students' sense of confidence. Lauren's teacher told the group of parents how exciting it is to see the light that beams in children's eyes when they start decoding words. Both teachers had been polite to Melanie before, but they were con-siderably warmer after the note. Notes of thanks help establish a positive relationship between teachers, parents, and students.

Don't forget the people who often don't get a lot of feedback or appreciation: the librarian, music teacher, art teacher, bus driver, and cafeteria worker. They work together to make the school environment a good one, and a note could encourage and build a relationship with them as well.

parent-teacher conferences

Another way to keep in touch with your child's teacher is by going to the parent-teacher conference. Schools generally set aside a certain day for these conferences, but if there is a need or you want an update on your child's progress, you can request a meeting with your child's teacher at any time during the school year. Here are some guidelines for making it a productive time of working together:

Attend together. If possible, both parents should attend the conference. With both parents present, you get a more balanced picture of the child and his school situation, and the school sees you're a united front.

Ignore the butterflies and go anyway. Be aware that nervousness or anxiety may surface because you are meeting with someone you don't know who teaches your child every day and is "in charge." Realize that these feelings are normal. "Butterflies raced in my stomach before the conference with Jennifer's teachers," said Carolyn. "I was so nervous, I couldn't think of what I wanted to say. I was afraid the teacher was going to tell me Jennifer had a reading problem or talked too much or something. I didn't know what she was going to say, and I didn't know if I really wanted to hear it."

For some people, such as Carolyn, the educational setting and jargon can be intimidating. If your own school days held painful experiences for you, old memories might surface and cause you to become defensive. The better you get to know the teacher, the less awkward the conferences will be.

Be prompt. This sounds like basic common courtesy that we all know, but teachers report that many parents are late for their conference and then expect to use some of the next parent's time. Be prepared by having asked your child in advance how things are going at school, what he likes best, and if he has any problems.

Try the sandwich approach. You may have something you're really upset about that's happened in the classroom or a problem you want to talk about. Sandwich these concerns and complaints between some positive comments about the class or the teacher's efforts. Generally, your concern will be better received by the teacher.

Be organized. You'll make better use of the brief time you have together. It might help to bring a list of a few questions such as:

- How is my child doing in class?

- Is she consistent about turning in classwork and homework?

- Does she pay attention? How is her behavior in class?

- How well does she get along with other children?

- What can be done at home to reinforce or support what you are doing here at school?

- Are there any learning activities you can suggest to be done at home?

Don't forget to listen. Conferences are a time for both parent and teacher to talk and listen. Be tactful but honest. Let the teacher know about any health problems, handicaps, or recent crises or changes at home that may affect your child's learning. In addition, share your goals for your child and what you're doing at home to help her. You can gain valuable insight into your child's development by listening carefully as the teacher describes how your child functions in class and how she is progressing both academically and socially.

troubleshooting

If there's a problem you're aware of, don't wait until your child fails before you call the teacher for a conference. Sometimes we (especially those of us who don't like conflict or confrontation) put things off and think, *Surely this is going to get better,* and then finally at the end of the year we realize it hasn't. In the meantime, our kid has lost major ground. Many problems kids have in the classroom don't resolve without intervention or help, so if you're concerned, write a note or call to request a parent-teacher conference.

Then, when you and the teacher meet together, troubleshoot to determine the problem. It might stem from a single situation in one class that negatively affects the whole school experience. It may be that your child is disorganized or feels overwhelmed. You as the parent see one side of the puzzle, and the teacher sees the other. Begin by sharing what's happening at home and describe what feedback you are getting from your child. (Often kids have more insight about a problem than we think.) Then ask, "What do you see here at school?" By putting your and the teacher's views together, you'll get a more complete picture of the situation.

Working together, you can identify the problem and discover solutions. Avoid approaching the discussion with a negative frame of mind, even if you think it's the teacher who has made a mistake. As one teacher said, "Some parents see a parent-teacher conference as a meeting of opposing forces." Instead, let your attitude be, "What can we do together to further the best interests of my child?"

Make sure you follow up on the conference. The teacher may suggest some home learning activities to strengthen your child's skills. Try your best to follow through on these suggestions and then get back with the teacher to share the results. Show interest in schoolwork, not just at a report-card conference or during crisis times but throughout the school year. Encourage your child to respect and cooperate with the teacher, to be attentive in class, and to communicate when a problem arises or help is needed.

You also might want to find some school-related activity you'd enjoy helping with. Most schools today are quite open to parental involvement and have lots of ways you can help, depending on your skills and interests. Some parents like to organize school carnivals, while others prefer to help in the computer room or library. Even working mothers and fathers can find time to become involved. One dad, who had a video and audio business, made a video that featured his child's school. The video was used to familiarize the community and new families with the school.

A mom I know loved gardening and mobilized her kids and their classmates to help plant flowers each spring in front of the school. You could volunteer to help with field trips; make materials for the classroom or assist in class; go to school one day a month and have lunch with your child in the cafeteria (and help as a monitor); participate in the local parent-teacher association; and attend school sports events, awards assemblies, musical programs, and art shows.

classroom observation

One of the best means of parent-teacher contact is visiting the classroom to observe how your child is being taught. You never know what is going on in the classroom, particularly the teacher's style and method of teaching, until you sit in the back of her room and watch the proceedings. This kind of firsthand observation helps you see how the teacher teaches and gives you a better grasp of how to help your child.[1]

When our oldest son was ready for first grade, he started out enthusiastic and excited about school, but it wasn't long before he was dreading it. He developed stomachaches in the morning and lost his enthusiasm. Besides asking for a conference with the teacher, I visited the classroom.

While I was reading to a small group of kids in the back part of the room, I noticed the teacher flicking a child on his head when he got the wrong answer to a math problem. It didn't happen once but several times. I couldn't believe it! Coupled with the negative atmosphere in the classroom and kids' anxiety (including our son's) over being the next victim, it was unlikely that any child could learn there. After exhausting every channel we could think of to work with the school, we moved our son to a different school. We were so glad we got to the bottom of things halfway through the year rather than at the end.

If you want to schedule a classroom observation, notify the principal ahead of time that you'd like to observe a class or classes to get a clearer picture of what's expected of your child so you can better help him at home. Arrive at the beginning of class rather than right in the middle so you don't disrupt instruction, and sit in the back. Before your visit, request a copy of the main textbooks so you can follow along with the class.

When you leave, don't forget to thank the teacher. One mother found that a good time to observe her child's classroom was when she came to the school to help with a birthday party or attend a PTA committee meeting. She would go a little early and watch the teacher and students interact and see how her child related to the other students in the class.

Encourage and pray for the teachers, administrators, and other students of your child's school. They need your support! Remember that many problems can be prevented or solved by keeping in touch. With good communication between you and your child's teacher, and your active interest and cooperation, school will be a much more positive experience for your child.

keeping kids learning
in the summer

Row after row of square gray markers covered a green Mississippi hill; towering over the Confederate and Union graves were huge magnolia trees. From this vantage point in the Vicksburg National Military Park, we gazed across the wide Mississippi River.

"Dad, look at the graves of all the soldiers who died in just the spring siege," Chris said, almost in a whisper. Suddenly, the number of men who had fought at Vicksburg was more than just an abstract fact in a history book. As we walked through trenches, crouched in replicas of shelters, and drove along the miles of battle lines across which Union and Confederate troops faced each other, we sensed the enormity of the struggle represented by only one vast Civil War battlefield.

Our three-hour visit to the Vicksburg Military Park was an experience that helped history come alive for our kids as no mere two-dimensional book could do. And it reminded us how enriching travel can be to a child's education.

An inexpensive guidebook to the park included a siege map, pictures, and a detailed description of the action that had taken place at various points along the miles-long siege lines. Now and then we would take turns reading aloud from the guidebook as we made our way along the sweeping battle lines.

As we drove along the battlefield drive, we read aloud signs and markers, and the inscriptions on the various battle monuments. We discovered things about the opposing forces, their leaders, and the position of their troops. We discussed the reasons for the Union thrust against Vicksburg, its importance to both sides, and the consequences of its ultimate fall. Bits and pieces of Civil War history our children had learned in school came together to form a clearer picture as they began to grasp the scope of the whole epic struggle.

There was plenty to touch and do. Poking our heads into every nook and cranny of the USS *Cairo* gave us a fascinating glimpse into the everyday life of the Civil War sailor. As we walked through the fields where Confederate fortifications had been erected, we could visualize the hand-to-hand confrontation that took place between the two armies. We could imagine the deafening roar as thousands of muskets and hundreds of cannons poured forth their deadly thunder.

Just as we discovered on our trip to Vicksburg, travel provides tremendous opportunities for your kids to learn history, natural science, geology, or other subjects. Seeing, hearing, and doing activities helps children understand what would otherwise be distant and abstract.

Travel doesn't have to be to some place faraway. There are many interesting history, science, and literary possibilities right in your own backyard! Many cities have hands-on science museums for young people, and each community has its own special land-marks. You can make the most of the outing by talking about what you are seeing. Let your kids share about their experiences by writing letters or postcards, drawing a picture about what they saw, and relating stories about the trip after they get home.

Before a planned vacation, call or e-mail the department of tourism of each state you will be visiting and request free information on areas of interest, especially living history centers. Involve your children in map study and historical research of the locale you're planning to visit. Then keep a travel journal or scrapbook as a family. Take along a notebook in which you can record the highlights of your trip, have your kids write or dictate their favorite things they saw and did, apply stickers, glue in postcards, and draw pictures of places you visited. Later, you can add photos, and you'll have a treasure when you look back on your adventures together. These days, many families are creating website scrapbooks of their travels so friends and relatives can experience the journey. If someone in your family is talented in simple web design, all of you can contribute, and the web-scrapbook will truly be a family creation.

travel box

There are many ways to keep your children happy and learning at the same time while traveling, whether it is on a short trip to Grandma's or a long trip through several states. Many people now have video or DVD players in their vehicle so the kids can watch movies, but I recommend limiting the movie-watching on vacation (just as you do normally at home) in favor of enriching activities. Start with a plastic container for a "travel box." In it, you can put pocket games of Yahtzee, Scrabble, Connect Four, and checkers. Auto bingo cards are fun to include, as well as two packs of cards for playing gin rummy, twenty-one, and other card games. Audiobooks and sing-along tapes are also good to include. You can check them out at the public library. Pens and paper are good for drawing, doodling, and playing dots, tic-tac-toe, and hangman. (Avoid crayons, as they will melt and make a big mess on your seats if the car gets hot.) Crossword puzzles, word finders, math puzzles, and new paperback books can round out your resources. After using it, keep the travel box packed and ready for the next trip.

These resources not only provide fun and help pass the long hours of riding but they also enhance children's learning. Family car trips can be a great time for togetherness rather than claustrophobia. Conflicts are minimized when boredom is banished!

Here are some more cures for the "backseat blues":

Geography: The first player begins by naming a country, state, city, or geographical area. The next player has to name a place that begins with the last letter of the one just given. If anyone repeats a location or cannot think of a new one, he is out. The last person still naming correctly wins the game.

Categories: To a clapped beat, each person names a brand of automobile, a species of animal, a type of fruit or vegetable, or an item from some other category you agree on. When a player fails to name a new item or repeats one already named, he is out of the game. The last one left wins.

Name That Tune: One person hums a familiar tune, and everyone else tries to guess what it is. Whoever guesses right gets to hum next!

Read-a-Thon: Take along a book the whole family will enjoy. Read one chapter a day aloud.

On our family trips, our kids also liked to read riddles from riddle books and try to guess the answers, make a list of the license plates from different states they saw (on a long trip, their goal was to spot a plate from every state in the Union), study the road maps and figure how far we still had to go, and play I Spy. Of course, you'll also need to take along your sense of humor and a big dose of flexibility when you travel with kids.

vacation time: progression or regression?

While some students today have year-round school with smaller chunks of breaks scattered throughout the school year, most still have an extended summer vacation. Between the time school ends for summer and resumes in the fall, many kids have too few learning experiences. Television watching and video game playing usually increase during the lazy, hazy days of summer. As their minds go out to pasture, many kids get rusty and return to school in September having forgotten much of the factual information they learned the year before.

Research has shown that children who have some at-home

learning activities during the summer months (even one a day) don't experience regression.[1] They can make progress and return as stronger students when school starts again.

Here are some ways to help your child *progress* rather than *regress* during those long, hot summer days at home:

Encourage doing at least one learning activity daily. You can use a calendar or an "activity bowl" out of which your child draws the name of one activity each day. These activities can combine fun and learning. For example, on the Fourth of July, the activity card might read, "See how many words you can make from the letters in INDEPENDENCE." On another day, it might say, "Make a list of major league baseball teams and put them into alphabetical order." You can fill your own activity bowl with ideas that work for your child's age and interests.

Find ways for your child to strengthen his skills over the summer break. Ask your child's teacher for ideas or check at educational resource stores in your area for suggestions. (These stores are not just for teachers. They stock great source materials for parents and often print a summer learning calendar for their customers.) You can also use activities from the math, reading, or writing chapters in this book.

Watch the Sunday paper for a kids' page, arts and crafts ideas section, and brain teasers. Clip these throughout the year and keep them on file for summer use. Some magazines also publish a learning idea page or an activity page for children that you can clip and store in your "Summer Learning Ideas" file. Include these in your activity bowl or on your summer learning calendar.

boost self-esteem and build relationships

Learning something new or doing a project together in the summer builds kids' confidence while providing happy memories. When they return to school in the fall, they can go back more confident and better able to tackle the new challenges that lie ahead during the school year.

Let summer be a time of building relationships. If you're working part-time or full-time and your schedule is as busy in the summer months as during the school year, be encouraged that even fifteen minutes a day spent in an enriching activity with you will have a tremendous impact on your child. One working mom I know decided that instead of going on a fancy family vacation on her two weeks off from work, she would have an "at-home" vacation. She designated one week for each of her daughters. They went to museums, a swim park, out to lunch together, shopping for school clothes—all while spending individual time with Mom.

Summer is a good time to interact with other families—because there is much to be learned from people in our neighborhood and community. Invite a family over for dinner and let your child help plan the menu and create the centerpiece. Or have a neighborhood block party or hamburger cookout and allow your child to make the invitations and help you decorate outdoors. Let each family bring a dish of food, play outdoor games, and enjoy the fellowship of your neighborhood.

making the most of summertime

Here are some spontaneous and inexpensive ways to enjoy the summer break:

- Plant and care for a small garden.

- Observe! In the daytime, lie out in the grass and watch clouds and their patterns. Ask your child, "What do you see?"

- Sprinkle bread crumbs in the yard. Wait quietly nearby and watch the birds eat.

- At night, lie outside and watch the stars. Have your child find certain stars and constellations, such as the North Star, the Big Dipper, and Orion.

- "Paint" the sidewalk with a big paintbrush and a bucket of water.

- Wash dolls, doll clothes, and toys with a small pail of water and liquid soap.

- Have a nature scavenger hunt in the backyard. Make a list of things to find: three rocks, a red and yellow flower, four different-shaped leaves, four different-sized sticks, and so on. Have a "rainy day" scavenger hunt in the house.

- Experiment with the wind using kites, pinwheels, bright balloons, and bubble-blowing liquid.

- Collect bugs and worms and study them under a magnifying glass.

- Have a cooking class for your child. Teach him to make a snack chosen from a children's cookbook. As you cook, talk about measurements as the child measures and stirs ingredients. Then the two of you can take your snacks, a cool drink, and a quilt out into the yard for an impromptu picnic.

games for learning

Many games exercise language, memory, and visual discrimination skills while the child is having fun, enjoying social interaction, and practicing making conversation. A game as simple as checkers involves planning and problem-solving skills important for school success. When your child has a friend over or just spends time with siblings, encourage them to stretch out on the floor and play a game.

Although there are many games to choose from, here are a few of the most popular, along with the skills they help improve:

- Hangman—problem solving, spelling

- Chutes and Ladders—counting, discrimination

- Scrabble, Scrabble for Juniors—language, vocabulary building

- Monopoly—planning, problem solving, math

- Racko—math

- Connect Four—planning, problem solving

summer reading motivation

Get a library card for each member of the family, and then take weekly trips to the library to keep your children's reading skills developing. A good incentive to keep your children reading during vacation time is the summer reading program provided by most libraries.

You can also set up your own family reading program with incentives based on the number of pages read. It is helpful to draw up a reading contract for each child to sign, in which each agrees in writing to read a certain number of pages each week. But be sure to make it fun, not work.

Our friends the Sargeants devised a successful summer reading program for their four children. Their youngest son, Ben, was to read two hundred pages a week, while Scott, Clayton, and Meghan were to read three hundred pages weekly. (The key is to set an age-appropriate goal that is challenging but doable.) Before any child began reading a selected book, Mom checked to make sure it was at the proper reading level. At the end of each week, she tallied the number of pages read by each child. For fulfilling the weekly quota, a child was awarded a trip to an ice cream shop for a sundae; for being on course for four weeks in a row, a child received an all-expense-paid trip to a local pizza parlor that featured video games. For keeping up with the reading schedule all summer long, the industrious child was rewarded with a U.S. savings bond. This incentive program kept all four children reading every moment they weren't swimming, playing baseball, or playing with friends.

summer enrichment

Besides all of the wonderful summer camps available to youngsters today, most colleges and universities now offer summer enrichment opportunities for children of all ages, including teens. Specialty camps (for interests ranging from computers to sports), art institutes, music festivals, children's drama classes, student stage productions, and many other programs are offered to encourage the gifts and talents of an enormous variety of young people. Check with your local university for summer enrichment programs offered in your area.

For thousands of Americans, life is most stressful when children first get out of school and into their parents' hair. How will summer be for *your* family? Boring and frustrating, or exciting and fulfilling? With a little planning, summer vacation can be the most enjoyable and satisfying time of the year for your children. They can return to school in the fall rested and refreshed, full of enthusiasm, and ready for another year of learning.

learning, love, and family life

The door opened and my son dragged into the kitchen after losing a baseball game. Over a glass of orange juice, he shared his frustrations and disappointment, and I listened. Finally, before he got up to start his homework, I said with a hug, "I love you regardless. You're special and important to me."

"But we lost," he replied.

"And on other days, you'll have other chances. But I love you!"

Those words didn't erase the pain of losing, but I have found that when kids come home with a D or an F on a test, the disappointment of an athletic failure, or the pain of a social crisis that has shaken their world, it's a good opportunity for us as parents to affirm our support of them. When our kids are least successful and even least lovable, they especially need our unconditional love.

Do you love me
Or do you not?
You told me once
But I forgot.

—Anonymous

Kids need their homes to be places where they can bring their problems, hurts, and disappointments and be sure of finding understanding, acceptance, and security.

Too often in our achievement-oriented society, we unknowingly give our children our love and affirmation only when they please us by winning a place on the honor roll or presenting us with a sports victory. We are affectionate when they are being what we want them to be: the ideal son or daughter, the A-student, the "star player." By doing so, we subtly deliver the message, "I love you for what you *do* and *achieve*." This leads to exactly what we don't want to see in our kids: underachievement, cheating on exams, and the development of low self-esteem.

When they continually fail to measure up to their parents' unrealistic expectations of them, children end up feeling worthless and unlovable. But kids who are unconditionally loved, and encouraged but not pressured, have the courage to step out and risk failure by trying something new in school or work.

"The most important factor in the development of children is the quality of love in their family," a counselor told me once. "Children do not learn or mature if they are not loved."

connecting with your kids

Perhaps you've heard the expression that to kids, love is spelled T-I-M-E. "Connection is essentially linked to time spent together," said William Richard Ezell, a pastor and father in Illinois. "Time is like oxygen; there's a minimum amount that is necessary for survival." It's a prerequisite for love and it takes quantity as well as quality to develop warm and caring relationships, he added.[1]

Developing strong, loving, secure attachments with our babies and children promotes brain development. Kids learn best in the context of significant relationships. Yet one of the biggest problems facing families today is fragmentation, with parents going in their own directions and kids going in other directions, all busy with so many good activities that they may not have time to develop a family life together. The result is that we get disconnected or distanced from those we love the most. Often quantity time spent with parents and siblings is the solution when kids have problems in school or get stressed, burned out, and discouraged.

A recent study by the Family Research Council showed that parents spend 40 percent less time with their kids than they did twenty-five years ago.[2] Most of us can't quit our jobs, but we can reevaluate our priorities and ask ourselves every day, *What really matters? Ten or twenty years down the road, what's really going to count? What should I invest my time in? How about my children's time?* When you face a promotion that will increase your workload and time spent away from home, ask yourself if it's worth it. Meet together for a family discussion occasionally to talk about how you're feeling about time pressures.

As we help our kids navigate the education process, we want to keep academics in proper perspective and aim for a balance between schoolwork and other areas—emotional, intellectual, physical, spiritual, and relational.

Your children's relationship with you is crucial to their education. Dr. Margie Golick, referring to what children need to know to become successful learners in school, says:

> *Many of the pleasures of learning and living come from relationships with other people. A child will be receptive to the teacher's teaching only if he has learned to care about the adults in his world. This kind of caring grows out of his own experiences of being cared about and respected and enjoyed.*[3]

From the beginning, by example perhaps more than by word, we teach attitudes, values, and habits that help shape our children's character now and throughout life. Children really do learn what they live at home! With the tools you've gained in this book and your innate love for your kids, the sky's the limit on what they can accomplish and learn.

notes

chapter 2: a stable home environment

1. "stability," *Webster's College Dictionary* (New York: Barnes and Noble, Inc., 2003), p. 887.
2. Vicky Mlyniec, "Reading, Writing, and Relaxation: How Slowing Down Speeds Learning," *Family Circle*, September 2, 2003, p. 80.
3. Dr. Dale Jordan (learning specialist and education professor, University of Arkansas), in discussion with the author.
4. Ohio State University fact sheet, "Children and Stress: Are You Pushing Your Child Too Hard?" http://ohioline.osu.edu/hyg-fact/5000/5152.html.
5. Dr. Eugene Walker (director of pediatric psychology training, University of Oklahoma Medical School), in discussion with the author.
6. Charlotte Sawtelle, *Learning Is a Family Affair* (Portland, Maine: Department of Educational and Cultural Services, 1984), p. 10.
7. Dr. Dale Jordan (learning specialist and education professor, University of Arkansas), in discussion with the author.
8. The author thanks family therapist Rhana Robison for her suggestions in this section.
9. Timothy S. Stuart and Cheryl Bostrom, *Children at Promise: 9 Principles to Help Kids Thrive in an At Risk World* (San Francisco: Jossey-Bass, 2003), p. 17.
10. "Family Problems: How They're Affecting Classrooms," *Learning*, January 1986.

chapter 3: turning your preschooler on to learning

1. Kaiser Family Foundation study, October 2003, www.kff.org/entmedia/3378.cfm.

2. Harry F. Waters, "What TV Does to Kids," *Newsweek*, February 21, 1977, p. 63.
3. Kaiser Family Foundation study.
4. The author is indebted to Margaret Loeffler for her insights on pretend play and child development.
5. William J. Bennett, *What Works: Research About Teaching and Learning* (Washington: United States Department of Education, 1986), p. 14.
6. Bennett, p. 25.
7. Jim Trelease, *The Read-Aloud Handbook* (New York: Penguin, 1986).
8. Gladys Hunt, *Honey for a Child's Heart* (Grand Rapids, Mich.: Zondervan, 1974).
9. My thanks to Candy Snowbarger for the Sticky, Smelly, and Color Walk ideas she shared with me when my kids were young.

chapter 4: raising readers

1. NAEP study, in *Engaging Young Readers: Promoting Achievement and Motivation*, ed. Linda Baker, Mariam Jean Dreher, and John T. Guthrie (New York: Guilford Press, 2000).
2. NAEP study (Washington: United States Department of Education, September, 1985).
3. William J. Bennett, *What Works: Research About Teaching and Learning* (Washington: United States Department of Education, 1986), p. 15.
4. Marie Winn, *Unplugging the Plug-In Drug* (New York: Viking Press, 1987), p. 58.

chapter 5: raising writers

1. Donald Graves and Virginia Stuart, *Write from the Start: Tapping Your Child's Natural Writing Ability* (New York: Dutton, 1985), p. 193.
2. Dr. Judy Abbott (education professor, University of West Virginia), in discussion with the author.
3. William J. Bennett, *What Works: Research About Teaching and*

Learning (Washington: United States Department of Education, 1986), p. 14.

chapter 6: music and your child's learning

1. National Association for Music Education website, http://www.menc.org/networks/boosters/bssm/intro.hml (accessed January 9, 2004).
2. From "Music and Your Child," a message delivered at the American Music Conference, 1988.
3. Dr. Gordon Shaw (professor of physics, University of California at Irvine), in discussion with the author.
4. From "Music and Your Child," a message delivered at the American Music Conference, 1988.

chapter 7: developing math skills

1. Claudia Zaslavsky, Preparing Young Children for Math: A Book of Games (New York: Schocken Books, 1979), p. xii.
2. "Math," Life, July 1993, p. 50.
3. Margie Golick, Deal Me In: The Use of Playing Cards in Teaching and Learning (New York: Simon & Schuster, 1981), p. 22.
4. Golick, p. 9.

chapter 8: encouraging good study habits

1. Dr. Dale Jordan (learning specialist and education professor, University of Arkansas), in discussion with the author.

chapter 9: helping your child retain information

1. Mel Levine, A Mind at a Time (New York: Simon & Schuster, 2002), p. 17.

chapter 10: the parent-teacher connection

1. William J. Bennett, *What Works: Research About Teaching and Learning* (Washington: United States Department of Education, 1986), p. 19.

chapter 11: keeping kids learning in the summer

1. William J. Bennett, *What Works: Research About Teaching and Learning* (Washington: United States Department of Education, 1986), p. 48.

chapter 12: learning, love, and family life

1. William Richard Ezell, "Finding Time to Connect," *Living with Teenagers*, September 1996, p. 10.
2. Ezell, p. 11.
3. Margie Golick, *Deal Me In: The Use of Playing Cards in Teaching and Learning* (New York: Simon & Schuster, 1981), p. 4.

recommended reading

Brazelton, T. Berry. *Touchpoints: Your Child's Emotional and Behavioral Development.* Cambridge, Mass.: Perseus, 1992.

Campbell, Don G. *The Mozart Effect for Children: Awakening Your Child's Mind, Health, and Creativity with Music.* New York: HarperCollins, 2000.

Campbell, Ross. *How to Really Love Your Child.* Colorado Springs, Colo.: Cook Communications, 2004.

Campbell, Ross. *How to Really Love Your Teen.* Colorado Springs, Colo.: Cook Communications, 2004.

Curry, Cyndi Lamb. *Keeping Your Kids Afloat When It Feels Like You're Sinking.* Ventura, Calif.: Regal, 2002.

Dobson, James. *New Hide or Seek: Building Confidence in Your Child.* Ada, Mich.: Revell, 2002.

Eisenberg, Arlene. *What to Expect the Toddler Years.* New York: Workman, 1996.

Elkind, David. *The Hurried Child: Growing Up Too Fast Too Soon.* Cambridge, Mass.: Perseus, 2001.

Fuller, Cheri. *Fearless: Building a Faith That Overcomes Your Fear.* Ada, Mich.: Revell, 2003.

Fuller, Cheri. *How to Grow a Young Music Lover.* Colorado Springs, Colo.: Shaw/WaterBrook, 2002.

Hunt, Gladys M. *Honey for a Child's Heart: The Imaginative Use of Books in Family Life.* Grand Rapids, Mich.: Zondervan, 2002.

Leman, Kevin. *Making Children Mind Without Losing Yours.* Ada, Mich.: Revell, 2000.

Lindskoog, Kathryn and Ranelda Mack Hunsicker. *How to Grow a Young Reader: A Parent's Guide to Books for Kids.* Colorado Springs, Colo.: Shaw/WaterBrook, 1999.

Stuart, Timothy S. and Cheryl G. Bostrom. *Children at Promise: 9 Principles to Help Kids Thrive in an At-Risk World.* San Francisco: Jossey-Bass, 2003.

Trelease, Jim. *The Read-Aloud Handbook.* New York: Penguin, 2001.

about the author

Cheri Fuller is an award-winning author, a speaker, and the mother of three grown children. She was selected as Oklahoma Mother of the Year for 2004. Her thirty published books include *The Mom You're Meant to Be*, *Extraordinary Kids* (coauthored with Louise Tucker Jones), *How to Grow a Young Music Lover*, *365 Ways to Develop Your Child's Values*, *Raising Motivated Kids*, and *Talkers, Watchers, and Doers*. Cheri speaks to parents, teachers, mothers' groups, and women's groups both in the U.S. and internationally, and she has appeared on national radio and TV programs such as *Focus on the Family* and *At-Home Live*. Hundreds of her articles have appeared in *Family Circle*, *ParentLife*, *Guideposts*, *Focus on the Family*, *Living with Teenagers*, and *CHILD*. She lives with her husband, Holmes, in Oklahoma.

For other resources as well as information about Cheri's speaking engagements, visit her website at www.cherifuller.com.

Other books in the SCHOOL SAVVY KIDS series by Cheri Fuller.

Talkers, Watchers, and Doers

Create a tailor-made learning environment for each of your children, equipping them with specialized study skills to match their unique personalities.
1-57683-599-5

Raising Motivated Kids

Packed with dozens of helpful hints, this book will show you how to turn your parental insight into powerful motivation to help your kids succeed in life.
1-57683-601-0

To get your copies, visit your local bookstore.